CW01081136

# MEMOIRS OF MARGUERITE DE VALOIS

# MEMOIRS OF MARGUERITE DE VALOIS

Marguerite de Valois

MEMOIRS OF MARGUERITE DE VALOIS

Published in the United States by IndyPublish.com
McLean, Virginia

ISBN 1-4043-2020-2 (hardcover)
ISBN 1-4043-2021-0 (paperback)

# TRANSLATOR'S PREFACE.

The Memoirs, of which a new translation is now presented to the public, are the undoubted composition of the celebrated princess whose name they bear, the contemporary of our Queen Elizabeth; of equal abilities with her, but of far unequal fortunes. Both Elizabeth and Marguerite had been bred in the school of adversity; both profited by it, but Elizabeth had the fullest opportunity of displaying her acquirements in it. Queen Elizabeth met with trials and difficulties in the early part of her life, and closed a long and successful reign in the happy possession of the good-will and love of her subjects. Queen Marguerite, during her whole life, experienced little else besides mortification and disappointment; she was suspected and hated by both Protestants and Catholics, with the latter of whom, though, she invariably joined in communion, yet was she not in the least inclined to persecute or injure the former. Elizabeth amused herself with a number of suitors, but never submitted to the yoke of matrimony. Marguerite, in compliance with the injunctions of the Queen her mother, and King Charles her brother, married Henri, King of Navarre, afterwards Henri IV. of France, for whom she had no inclination; and this union being followed by a mutual indifference and dislike, she readily consented to dissolve it; soon after which event she saw a princess, more fruitful but less prudent, share the throne of her ancestors, of whom she was the only representative. Elizabeth was polluted with the blood of her cousin, the Queen of Scots, widow of Marguerite's eldest brother. Marguerite saved many Huguenots from the massacre of St. Bartholomew's Day, and, according to Brantome, the life of the King, her husband, whose name was on the list of the proscribed. To close this parallel, Elizabeth began early to govern a kingdom, which she ruled through the course of her long life with severity, yet gloriously, and with success. Marguerite, after the death of the Queen her mother and her brothers, though sole heiress of the House of Valois, was, by the

Salic law, excluded from all pretensions to the Crown of France; and though for the greater part of her life shut up in a castle, surrounded by rocks and mountains, she has not escaped the shafts of obloquy.

The Translator has added some notes, which give an account of such places as are mentioned in the Memoirs, taken from the itineraries of the time, but principally from the "Geographie Universelle" of Vosgien; in which regard is had to the new division of France into departments, as well as to the ancient one of principalities, archbishoprics, bishoprics, generalities, chatellenies, balliages, duchies, seigniories, etc.

In the composition of her Memoirs, Marguerite has evidently adopted the epistolary form, though the work came out of the French editor's hand divided into three (as they are styled) books; these three books, or letters, the Translator has taken the liberty of subdividing into twenty- one, and, at the head of each of them, he has placed a short table of the contents. This is the only liberty he has taken with the original Memoirs, the translation itself being as near as the present improved state of our language could be brought to approach the unpolished strength and masculine vigour of the French of the age of Henri IV.

This translation is styled a new one, because, after the Translator had made some progress in it, he found these Memoirs had already been made English, and printed, in London, in the year 1656, thirty years after the first edition of the French original. This translation has the following title: "The grand Cabinet Counsels unlocked; or, the most faithful Transaction of Court Affairs, and Growth and Continuance of the Civil Wars in France, during the Reigns of Charles the last, Henry III., and Henry IV., commonly called the Great. Most excellently written, in the French Tongue, by Margaret de Valois, Sister to the two first Kings, and Wife of the last. Faithfully translated by Robert Codrington, Master of Arts;" and again as "Memorials of Court Affairs," etc., London, 1658.

The Memoirs of Queen Marguerite contained the secret history of the Court of France during the space of seventeen years, from 1565 to 1582, and they end seven years before Henri III., her brother, fell by the hands of Clement, the monk; consequently, they take in no part of the reign of Henri IV. (as Mr. Codrington has asserted in his title-page), though they relate many particulars of the early part of his life.

Marguerite's Memoirs include likewise the history nearly of the first half of her own life, or until she had reached the twenty-ninth year of her age; and as she died in 1616, at the age of sixty-three years, there remain thirty-four years of her life, of which little is known. In 1598, when she was forty-five years old, her marriage with Henri was dissolved by mutual consent,—she declaring that she had no other wish than to give him content, and preserve the peace of the kingdom; making it her request, according to Brantome, that the King would favour her with his protection, which, as her letter expresses, she hoped to enjoy during the rest of her life. Sully says she stipulated only for an establishment and the payment of her debts, which were granted. After Henri, in 1610, had fallen a victim to the furious fanaticism of the monk Ravaillac, she lived to see the kingdom brought into the greatest confusion by the bad government of the Queen Regent, Marie de Medici, who suffered herself to be directed by an Italian woman she had brought over with her, named Leonora Galligai. This woman marrying a Florentine, called Concini, afterwards made a marshal of France, they jointly ruled the kingdom, and became so unpopular that the marshal was assassinated, and the wife, who had been qualified with the title of Marquise d'Ancre, burnt for a witch. This happened about the time of Marguerite's decease.

It has just before been mentioned how little has been handed down to these times respecting Queen Marguerite's history. The latter part of her life, there is reason to believe, was wholly passed at a considerable distance from Court, in her retirement (so it is called, though it appears to have been rather her prison) at the castle of Usson. This castle, rendered famous by her long residence in it, has been demolished since the year 1634. It was built on a mountain, near a little town of the same name, in that part of France called Auvergne, which now constitutes part of the present Departments of the Upper Loire and Puy- de-Dome, from a river and mountain so named. These Memoirs appear to have been composed in this retreat. Marguerite amused herself likewise, in this solitude, in composing verses, and there are specimens still remaining of her poetry. These compositions she often set to music, and sang them herself, accompanying her voice with the lute, on which she played to perfection. Great part of her time was spent in the perusal of the Bible and books of piety, together with the works of the best authors she could procure. Brantome assures us that Marguerite spoke the Latin tongue with purity and elegance; and it appears, from her Memoirs, that she had read Plutarch with attention.

Marguerite has been said to have given in to the gallantries to which the Court of France was, during her time, but too much addicted; but, though the Translator is obliged to notice it, he is far from being inclined to give any credit to a romance entitled, "Le Divorce Satyrique; ou, les Amours de la Reyne Marguerite de Valois," which is written in the person of her husband, and bears on the title-page these initials: D. R. H. Q. M.; that is to say, "du Roi Henri Quatre, Mari." This work professes to give a relation of Marguerite's conduct during her residence at the castle of Usson; but it contains so many gross absurdities and indecencies that it is undeserving of attention, and appears to have been written by some bitter enemy, who has assumed the character of her husband to traduce her memory.

["Le Divorce Satyrique" is said to have been written by Louise Marguerite de Lorraine, Princesse de Conti, who is likewise the reputed author of "The Amours of Henri IV.," disguised under the name of Alcander. She was the daughter of the Due de Guise, assassinated at Blois in 1588, and was born the year her father died. She married Francois, Prince de Conti, and was considered one of the most ingenious and accomplished persons belonging to the French Court in the age of Louis XIII. She was left a widow in 1614, and died in 1631.]

M. Pierre de Bourdeille, Seigneur de Brantome, better known by the name of Brantome, wrote the Memoirs of his own times. He was brought up in the Court of France, and lived in it during the reigns of Marguerite's father and brothers, dying at the advanced age of eighty or eighty-four years, but in what year is not certainly known. He has given anecdotes—

[The author of the "Tablettes de France," and "Anecdotes des Rois de France," thinks that Marguerite alludes to Brantome's "Anecdotes" in the beginning of her first letter, where she says: "I should commend your work much more were I myself not so much praised in it." (According to the original: "Je louerois davantage votre oeuvre, si elle ne me louoit tant.") If so, these letters were addressed to Brantome, and not to the Baron de la Chataigneraie, as mentioned in the Preface to the French edition. In Letter I. mention is made of Madame de Dampierre, whom Marguerite styles the aunt of the person the letter is addressed to. She was dame d'honneur, or lady of the bedchamber, to the Queen of Henri III., and Brantome, speaking of her, calls her his aunt. Indeed, it is not a matter of any consequence to whom these Memoirs were addressed; it is, however, remarkable that Louis XIV. used the same words to Boileau, after hearing him read his celebrated epistle upon the famous Passage of the Rhine; and yet Louis was no reader, and is not supposed to have adopted them from these Memoirs. The thought is, in reality, fine, but might easily suggest itself to any other. "Cela est beau," said the monarch, "et je vous louerois davantage, si vous m'aviez moins loue." (The poetry is excellent, and I should praise you more had you praised me less.)]

of the life of Marguerite, written during her before-mentioned retreat, when she was, as he says ("fille unique maintenant restee, de la noble maison de France"), the only survivor of her illustrious house. Brantome praises her excellent beauty in a long string of laboured hyperboles. Ronsard, the Court poet, has done the same in a poem of considerable length, wherein he has exhausted all his wit and fancy. From what they have said, we may collect that Marguerite was graceful in her person and figure, and remarkably happy in her choice of dress and ornaments to set herself off to the most advantage; that her height was above the middle size, her shape easy, with that due proportion of plumpness which gives an appearance of majesty and comeliness. Her eyes were full, black, and sparkling; she had bright, chestnut-coloured hair, and a complexion fresh and blooming. Her skin was delicately white, and her neck admirably well formed; and this so generally admired beauty, the fashion of dress, in her time, admitted of being fully displayed.

Such was Queen Marguerite as she is portrayed, with the greatest luxuriance of colouring, by these authors. To her personal charms were added readiness of wit, ease and gracefulness of speech, and great affability and courtesy of manners. This description of Queen Marguerite cannot be dismissed without observing, if only for the sake of keeping the fashion of the present times with her sex in countenance, that, though she had hair, as has been already described, becoming her, and sufficiently ornamental in itself, yet she occasionally called in the aid of wigs. Brantome's words are: "l'artifice de perruques bien gentiment faconnees."

[Ladies in the days of Ovid wore periwigs. That poet says to Corinna:

> "Nunc tibi captivos mittet Germania crines;
> Culta triumphatae munere gentis eris."

(Wigs shall from captive Germany be sent;
'Tis with such spoils your head you ornament.)

These, we may conclude, were flaxen, that being the prevailing coloured hair of the Germans at this day. The Translator has met with a further account of Marguerite's head-dress, which describes her as wearing a velvet bonnet ornamented with pearls and diamonds, and surmounted with a plume of feathers.]

I shall conclude this Preface with a letter from Marguerite to Brantome; the first, he says, he received from her during her adversity ('son adversite' are his words),—being, as he expresses it, so ambitious ('presomptueux') as to have sent to inquire concerning her health, as she was the daughter and sister of the Kings, his masters. ("D'avoir envoye scavoir de ses nouvelles, mais quoy elle estoit fille et soeur de mes roys.")

The letter here follows: "From the attention and regard you have shown me (which to me appears less strange than it is agreeable), I find you still preserve that attachment you have ever had to my family, in a recollection of these poor remains which have escaped its wreck. Such as I am, you will find me always ready to do you service, since I am so happy as to discover that my fortune has not been able to blot out my name from the memory of my oldest friends, of which number you are one. I have heard that, like me, you have chosen a life of retirement, which I esteem those happy who can enjoy, as God, out of His great mercy, has enabled me to do for these last five years; having placed me, during these times of trouble, in an ark of safety, out of the reach, God be thanked, of storms. If, in my present situation, I am able to serve my friends, and you more especially, I shall be found entirely disposed to it, and with the greatest good-will."

There is such an air of dignified majesty in the foregoing letter, and, at the same time, such a spirit of genuine piety and resignation, that it cannot but give an exalted idea of Marguerite's character, who appears superior to ill-fortune and great even in her distress. If, as I doubt not, the reader thinks the same, I shall not need to make an apology for concluding this Preface with it.

The following Latin verses, or call them, if you please, epigram, are of the composition of Barclay, or Barclaius, author of "Argenis," etc.

## ON MARGUERITE DE VALOIS, QUEEN OF NAVARRE.

Dear native land! and you, proud castles! say (Where grandsire,[1] father,[2] and three brothers[3] lay, Who each, in turn, the crown imperial wore), Me will you own, your daughter whom you bore? Me, once your greatest boast and chiefest pride, By Bourbon and Lorraine,[4] when sought a bride; Now widowed wife,[5] a queen without a throne, Midst rocks and mountains [6] wander I alone. Nor yet hath Fortune vented all her spite, But sets one up,[7] who now enjoys my right, Points to the boy,[8] who henceforth claims the throne And crown, a son of mine should call his own. But ah, alas! for me 'tis now too late [9] To strive 'gainst Fortune and contend with Fate; Of those I slighted, can I beg relief [10] No; let me die the victim of my grief. And can I then be justly said to live? Dead in estate, do I then yet survive? Last of the name, I carry to the grave All the remains the House of Valois have.

1. Francois I.
2. Henri II.
3. Francois II., Charles IX., and Henri III.
4. Henri, King of Navarre, and Henri, Duc de Guise.
5. Alluding to her divorce from Henri IV..

6. The castle of Usson

7. Marie de' Medici, whom Henri married after his divorce from Marguerite.

8. Louis XIII., the son of Henri and his queen, Marie de' Medici.

9. Alluding to the differences betwixt Marguerite and Henri, her husband.

10. This is said with allusion to the supposition that she was rather inclined to favour the suit of the Due de Guise and reject Henri for a husband.

# LETTER I.

*Introduction.—Anecdotes of Marguerite's Infancy.—Endeavours Used to Convert Her to the New Religion.—She Is Confirmed in Catholicism.— The Court on a Progress.—A Grand Festivity Suddenly Interrupted.— The Confusion in Consequence.*

I should commend your work much more were I myself less praised in it; but I am unwilling to do so, lest my praises should seem rather the effect of self-love than to be founded on reason and justice. I am fearful that, like Themistocles, I should appear to admire their eloquence the most who are most forward to praise me. It is the usual frailty of our sex to be fond of flattery. I blame this in other women, and should wish not to be chargeable with it myself. Yet I confess that I take a pride in being painted by the hand of so able a master, however flattering the likeness may be. If I ever were possessed of the graces you have assigned to me, trouble and vexation render them no longer visible, and have even effaced them from my own recollection. So that I view myself in your Memoirs, and say, with old Madame de Rendan, who, not having consulted her glass since her husband's death, on seeing her own face in the mirror of another lady, exclaimed, "Who is this?" Whatever my friends tell me when they see me now, I am inclined to think proceeds from the partiality of their affection. I am sure that you yourself, when you consider more impartially what you have said, will be induced to believe, according to these lines of Du Bellay:

> "C'est chercher Rome en Rome,
> Et rien de Rome en Rome ne trouver."

('Tis to seek Rome, in Rome to go,
And Rome herself at Rome not know.)

But as we read with pleasure the history of the Siege of Troy, the magnificence of
Athens, and other splendid cities, which once flourished, but are now so entirely
destroyed that scarcely the spot whereon they stood can be traced, so you please
yourself with describing these excellences of beauty which are no more, and which
will be discoverable only in your writings.

If you had taken upon you to contrast Nature and Fortune, you could not have
chosen a happier theme upon which to descant, for both have made a trial of their
strength on the subject of your Memoirs. What Nature did, you had the evidence
of your own eyes to vouch for, but what was done by Fortune, you know only
from hearsay; and hearsay, I need not tell you, is liable to be influenced by ignorance or malice, and, therefore, is not to be depended on. You will for that reason, I make no doubt, be pleased to receive these Memoirs from the hand which
is most interested in the truth of them.

I have been induced to undertake writing my Memoirs the more from five or six
observations which I have had occasion to make upon your work, as you appear
to have been misinformed respecting certain particulars. For example, in that part
where mention is made of Pau, and of my journey in France; likewise where you
speak of the late Marechal de Biron, of Agen, and of the sally of the Marquis de
Camillac from that place.

These Memoirs might merit the honourable name of history from the truths contained in them, as I shall prefer truth to embellishment. In fact, to embellish my
story I have neither leisure nor ability; I shall, therefore, do no more than give a
simple narration of events. They are the labours of my evenings, and will come to
you an unformed mass, to receive its shape from your hands, or as a chaos on
which you have already thrown light. Mine is a history most assuredly worthy to
come from a man of honour, one who is a true Frenchman, born of illustrious
parents, brought up in the Court of the Kings my father and brothers, allied in
blood and friendship to the most virtuous and accomplished women of our times,
of which society I have had the good fortune to be the bond of union.

I shall begin these Memoirs in the reign of Charles IX., and set out with the first
remarkable event of my life which fell within my remembrance. Herein I follow
the example of geographical writers, who, having described the places within their
knowledge, tell you that all beyond them are sandy deserts, countries without
inhabitants, or seas never navigated. Thus I might say that all prior to the com-

mencement of these Memoirs was the barrenness of my infancy, when we can only be said to vegetate like plants, or live, like brutes, according to instinct, and not as human creatures, guided by reason. To those who had the direction of my earliest years I leave the task of relating the transactions of my infancy, if they find them as worthy of being recorded as the infantine exploits of Themistocles and Alexander,—the one exposing himself to be trampled on by the horses of a charioteer, who would not stop them when requested to do so, and the other refusing to run a race unless kings were to enter the contest against him. Amongst such memorable things might be related the answer I made the King my father, a short time before the fatal accident which deprived France of peace, and our family of its chief glory. I was then about four or five years of age, when the King, placing me on his knee, entered familiarly into chat with me. There were, in the same room, playing and diverting themselves, the Prince de Joinville, since the great and unfortunate Duc de Guise, and the Marquis de Beaupreau, son of the Prince de la Roche-sur-Yon, who died in his fourteenth year, and by whose death his country lost a youth of most promising talents. Amongst other discourse, the King asked which of the two Princes that were before me I liked best. I replied, "The Marquis." The King said, "Why so? He is not the handsomest." The Prince de Joinville was fair, with light-coloured hair, and the Marquis de Beaupreau brown, with dark hair. I answered, "Because he is the best behaved; whilst the Prince is always making mischief, and will be master over everybody."

This was a presage of what we have seen happen since, when the whole Court was infected with heresy, about the time of the Conference of Poissy. It was with great difficulty that I resisted and preserved myself from a change of religion at that time. Many ladies and lords belonging to Court strove to convert me to Huguenotism. The Duc d'Anjou, since King Henri III. of France, then in his infancy, had been prevailed on to change his religion, and he often snatched my "Hours" out of my hand, and flung them into the fire, giving me Psalm Books and books of Huguenot prayers, insisting on my using them. I took the first opportunity to give them up to my governess, Madame de Curton, whom God, out of his mercy to me, caused to continue steadfast in the Catholic religion. She frequently took me to that pious, good man, the Cardinal de Tournon, who gave me good advice, and strengthened me in a perseverance in my religion, furnishing me with books and chaplets of beads in the room of those my brother Anjou took from me and burnt.

Many of my brother's most intimate friends had resolved on my ruin, and rated me severely upon my refusal to change, saying it proceeded from a childish obstinacy; that if I had the least understanding, and would listen, like other discreet persons, to the sermons that were preached, I should abjure my uncharitable bigotry; but I was, said they, as foolish as my governess. My brother Anjou added threats, and said the Queen my mother would give orders that I should be whipped. But this he said of his own head, for the Queen my mother did not, at that time, know of the errors he had embraced. As soon as it came to her knowledge, she took him to task, and severely reprimanded his governors, insisting upon their correcting him, and instructing him in the holy and ancient religion of his forefathers, from which she herself never swerved. When he used those menaces, as I have before related, I was a child seven or eight years old, and at that tender age would reply to him, "Well, get me whipped if you can; I will suffer whipping, and even death, rather than be damned."

I could furnish you with many other replies of the like kind, which gave proof of the early ripeness of my judgment and my courage; but I shall not trouble myself with such researches, choosing rather to begin these Memoirs at the time when I resided constantly with the Queen my mother.

Immediately after the Conference of Poissy, the civil wars commenced, and my brother Alencon and myself, on account of our youth, were sent to Amboise, whither all the ladies of the country repaired to us.

With them came your aunt, Madame de Dampierre, who entered into a firm friendship with me, which was never interrupted until her death broke it off. There was likewise your cousin, the Duchesse de Rais, who had the good fortune to hear there of the death of her brute of a husband, killed at the battle of Dreux. The husband I mean was the first she had, named M. d'Annebaut, who was unworthy to have for a wife so accomplished and charming a woman as your cousin. She and I were not then so intimate friends as we have become since, and shall ever remain. The reason was that, though older than I, she was yet young, and young girls seldom take much notice of children, whereas your aunt was of an age when women admire their innocence and engaging simplicity.

I remained at Amboise until the Queen my mother was ready to set out on her grand progress, at which time she sent for me to come to her Court, which I did not quit afterwards.

Of this progress I will not undertake to give you a description, being still so young that, though the whole is within my recollection, yet the particular passages of it appear to me but as a dream, and are now lost. I leave this task to others, of riper years, as you were yourself. You can well remember the magnificence that was displayed everywhere, particularly at the baptism of my nephew, the Duc de Lorraine, at Bar-le- Duc; at the meeting of M. and Madame de Savoy, in the city of Lyons; the interview at Bayonne betwixt my sister, the Queen of Spain, the Queen my mother, and King Charles my brother. In your account of this interview you would not forget to make mention of the noble entertainment given by the Queen my mother, on an island, with the grand dances, and the form of the salon, which seemed appropriated by nature for such a purpose, it being a large meadow in the middle of the island, in the shape of an oval, surrounded on every aide by tall spreading trees. In this meadow the Queen my mother had disposed a circle of niches, each of them large enough to contain a table of twelve covers. At one end a platform was raised, ascended by four steps formed of turf. Here their Majesties were seated at a table under a lofty canopy. The tables were all served by troops of shepherdesses dressed in cloth of gold and satin, after the fashion of the different provinces of France. These shepherdesses, during the passage of the superb boats from Bayonne to the island, were placed in separate bands, in a meadow on each side of the causeway, raised with turf; and whilst their Majesties and the company were passing through the great salon, they danced. On their passage by water, the barges were followed by other boats, having on board vocal and instrumental musicians, habited like Nereids, singing and playing the whole time. After landing, the shepherdesses I have mentioned before received the company in separate troops, with songs and dances, after the fashion and accompanied by the music of the provinces they represented,— the Poitevins playing on bagpipes; the Provencales on the viol and cymbal; the Burgundians and Champagners on the hautboy, bass viol, and tambourine; in like manner the Bretons and other provincialists. After the collation was served and the feast at an end, a large troop of musicians, habited like satyrs, was seen to come out of the opening of a rock, well lighted up, whilst nymphs were descending from the top in rich habits, who, as they came down, formed into a grand dance, when, lo! fortune no longer favouring this brilliant festival, a sudden storm of rain came on, and all were glad to get off in the boats and make for town as fast as they could. The confusion in consequence of this precipitate retreat afforded as much matter to laugh at the next day as the splendour of the entertainment had excited admiration. In short, the festivity of this day was not, forgotten, on one account or the other, amidst the variety of the like nature which succeeded it in the course of this progress.

## LETTER II.

*Message from the Duc d'Anjou, Afterwards Henri III., to King Charles His Brother and the Queen-mother.—Her Fondness for Her Children.—Their Interview.—Anjou's Eloquent Harangue.—The Queen-mother's Character. Discourse of the Duc d'Anjou with Marguerite.—She Discovers Her Own Importance.—Engages to Serve Her Brother Anjou.—Is in High Favour with the Queenmother.*

At the time my magnanimous brother Charles reigned over France, and some few years after our return from the grand progress mentioned in my last letter, the Huguenots having renewed the war, a gentleman, despatched from my brother Anjou (afterwards Henri III. of France), came to Paris to inform the King and the Queen my mother that the Huguenot army was reduced to such an extremity that he hoped in a few days to force them to give him battle. He added his earnest wish for the honour of seeing them at Tours before that happened, so that, in case Fortune, envying him the glory he had already achieved at so early an age, should, on the so much looked-for day, after the good service he had done his religion and his King, crown the victory with his death, he might not have cause to regret leaving this world without the satisfaction of receiving their approbation of his conduct from their own mouths, a satisfaction which would be more valuable, in his opinion, than the trophies he had gained by his two former victories.

I leave to your own imagination to suggest to you the impression which such a message from a dearly beloved son made on the mind of a mother who doted on all her children, and was always ready to sacrifice her own repose, nay, even her life, for their happiness.

She resolved immediately to set off and take the King with her. She had, besides myself, her usual small company of female attendants, together with Mesdames de Rais and de Sauves. She flew on the wings of maternal affection, and reached Tours in three days and a half. A journey from Paris, made with such precipitation, was not unattended with accidents and some inconveniences, of a nature to occasion much mirth and laughter. The poor Cardinal de Bourbon, who never quitted her, and whose temper of mind, strength of body, and habits of life were ill suited to encounter privations and hardships, suffered greatly from this rapid journey.

We found my brother Anjou at Plessis-les-Tours, with the principal officers of his army, who were the flower of the princes and nobles of France. In their presence he delivered a harangue to the King, giving a detail of his conduct in the execution of his charge, beginning from the time he left the Court. His discourse was framed with so much eloquence, and spoken so gracefully, that it was admired by all present. It appeared matter of astonishment that a youth of sixteen should reason with all the gravity and powers of an orator of ripe years. The comeliness of his person, which at all times pleads powerfully in favour of a speaker, was in him set off by the laurels obtained in two victories. In short, it was difficult to say which most contributed to make him the admiration of all his hearers.

It is equally as impossible for me to describe in words the feelings of my mother on this occasion, who loved him above all her children, as it was for the painter to represent on canvas the grief of Iphigenia's father. Such an overflow of joy would have been discoverable in the looks and actions of any other woman, but she had her passions so much under the control of prudence and discretion that there was nothing to be perceived in her countenance, or gathered from her words, of what she felt inwardly in her mind. She was, indeed, a perfect mistress of herself, and regulated her discourse and her actions by the rules of wisdom and sound policy, showing that a person of discretion does upon all occasions only what is proper to be done. She did not amuse herself on this occasion with listening to the praises which issued from every mouth, and sanction them with her own approbation; but, selecting the chief points in the speech relative to the future conduct of the war, she laid them before the Princes and great lords, to be deliberated upon, in order to settle a plan of operations.

To arrange such a plan a delay of some days was requisite. During this interval, the Queen my mother walking in the park with some of the Princes, my brother Anjou begged me to take a turn or two with him in a retired walk. He then addressed me in the following words: "Dear sister, the nearness of blood, as well as our having been brought up together, naturally, as they ought, attach us to each other. You must already have discovered the partiality I have had for you above my brothers, and I think that I have perceived the same in you for me. We have been hitherto led to this by nature, without deriving any other advantage from it than the sole pleasure of conversing together. So far might be well enough for our childhood, but now we are no longer children. You know the high situation in which, by the favour of God and our good mother the Queen, I am here placed. You may be assured that, as you are the person in the world whom I love and esteem the most, you will always be a partaker of my advancement. I know you are not wanting in wit and discretion, and I am sensible you have it in your power to do me service with the Queen our mother, and preserve me in my present employments. It is a great point obtained for me, always to stand well in her favour. I am fearful that my absence may be prejudicial to that purpose, and I must necessarily be at a distance from Court. Whilst I am away, the King my brother is with her, and has it in his power to insinuate himself into her good graces. This I fear, in the end, may be of disservice to me. The King my brother is growing older every day. He does not want for courage, and, though he now diverts himself with hunting, he may grow ambitious, and choose rather to chase men than beasts; in such a case I must resign to him my commission as his lieu-tenant. This would prove the greatest mortification that could happen to me, and I would even prefer death to it. Under such an apprehension I have considered of the means of prevention, and see none so feasible as having a confidential person about the Queen my mother, who shall always be ready to espouse and support my cause. I know no one so proper for that purpose as yourself, who will be, I doubt not, as attentive to my interest as I should be myself. You have wit, discre-tion, and fidelity, which are all that are wanting, provided you will be so kind as to undertake such a good office. In that case I shall have only to beg of you not to neglect attending her morning and evening, to be the first with her and the last to leave her. This will induce her to repose a confidence and open her mind to you.

"To make her the more ready to do this, I shall take every opportunity, to com-mend your good sense and understanding, and to tell her that I shall take it kind in her to leave off treating you as a child, which, I shall say, will contribute to her own comfort and satisfaction. I am well convinced that she will listen to my advice. Do you speak to her with the same confidence as you do to me, and be assured that she will approve of it. It will conduce to your own happiness to obtain her favour. You may do yourself service whilst you are labouring for my interest; and you may rest satisfied that, after God, I shall think I owe all the good fortune which may befall me to yourself."

This was entirely a new kind of language to me. I had hitherto thought of noth-ing but amusements, of dancing, hunting, and the like diversions; nay, I had never yet discovered any inclination of setting myself off to advantage by dress, and exciting an admiration of my person and figure. I had no ambition of any kind, and had been so strictly brought up under the Queen my mother that I scarcely durst speak before her; and if she chanced to turn her eyes towards me I trembled, for fear that I had done something to displease her. At the conclusion of my brother's harangue, I was half inclined to reply to him in the words of Moses, when he was spoken to from the burning bush: "Who am I, that I should go unto Pharaoh? Send, I pray thee, by the hand of him whom thou wilt send."

However, his words inspired me with resolution and powers I did not think myself possessed of before. I had naturally a degree of courage, and, as soon as I recovered from my astonishment, I found I was quite an altered person. His address pleased me, and wrought in me a confidence in myself; and I found I was become of more consequence than I had ever conceived I had been. Accordingly, I replied to him thus: "Brother, if God grant me the power of speaking to the Queen our mother as I have the will to do, nothing can be wanting for your service, and you may expect to derive all the good you hope from it, and from my solicitude and attention for your interest. With respect to my undertaking such a matter for you, you will soon perceive that I shall sacrifice all the pleasures in this world to my watchfulness for your service. You may perfectly rely on me, as there is no one that honours or regards you more than I do. Be well assured that I shall act for you with the Queen my mother as zealously as you would for yourself."

These sentiments were more strongly impressed upon my mind than the words I made use of were capable of conveying an idea of. This will appear more fully in my following letters.

As soon as we were returned from walking, the Queen my mother retired with me into her closet, and addressed the following words to me: "Your brother has been relating the conversation you have had together; he considers you no longer as a child, neither shall I. It will be a great comfort to me to converse with you as I would with your brother. For the future you will freely speak your mind, and have no apprehensions of taking too great a liberty, for it is what I wish." These words gave me a pleasure then which I am now unable to express. I felt a satisfaction and a joy which nothing before had ever caused me to feel. I now considered the pastimes of my childhood as vain amusements. I shunned the society of my former companions of the same age. I disliked dancing and hunting, which I thought beneath my attention. I strictly complied with her agreeable injunction, and never missed being with her at her rising in the morning and going to rest at night. She did me the honour, sometimes, to hold me in conversation for two and three hours at a time. God was so gracious with me that I gave her great satisfaction; and she thought she could not sufficiently praise me to those ladies who were about her. I spoke of my brother's affairs to her, and he was constantly apprised by me of her sentiments and opinion; so that he had every reason to suppose I was firmly attached to his interest.

# LETTER III.

*Le Guast.—His Character.—Anjou Affects to Be Jealous of the Guises.— Dissuades the Queen-mother from Reposing Confidence in Marguerite.— She Loses the Favour of the Queen-mother and Falls Sick.— Anjou's Hypocrisy.—He Introduces De Guise into Marguerite's Sick Chamber.—Marguerite Demanded in Marriage by the King of Portugal.— Made Uneasy on That Account.—Contrives to Relieve Herself.— The Match with Portugal Broken off..*

I continued to pass my time with the Queen my mother, greatly to my satisfaction, until after the battle of Moncontour. By the same despatch that brought the news of this victory to the Court, my brother, who was ever desirous to be near the Queen my mother, wrote her word that he was about to lay siege to St. Jean d'Angely, and that it would be necessary that the King should be present whilst it was going on.

She, more anxious to see him than he could be to have her near him, hastened to set out on the journey, taking me with her, and her customary train of attendants. I likewise experienced great joy upon the occasion, having no suspicion that any mischief awaited me. I was still young and without experience, and I thought the happiness I enjoyed was always to continue; but the malice of Fortune prepared for me at this interview a reverse that I little expected, after the fidelity with which I had discharged the trust my brother had reposed in me.

Soon after our last meeting, it seems, my brother Anjou had taken Le Guast to be near his person, who had ingratiated himself so far into his favour and confidence that he saw only with his eyes, and spoke but as he dictated. This evil-disposed man, whose whole life was one continued scene of wickedness, had perverted his mind and filled it with maxims of the most atrocious nature. He advised him to have no regard but for his own interest; neither to love nor put trust in any one; and not to promote the views or advantage of either brother or sister. These and other maxims of the like nature, drawn from tho school of Machiavelli, he was continually suggesting to him. He had so frequently inculcated them that they were strongly impressed on his mind, insomuch that, upon our arrival, when, after the first compliments, my mother began to open in my praise and express the attachment I had discovered for him, this was his reply, which he delivered with the utmost coldness:

"He was well pleased," he said, "to have succeeded in the request he had made to me; but that prudence directed us not to continue to make use of the same expedients, for what was profitable at one time might not be so at another." She asked him why he made that observation. This question afforded the opportunity he wished for, of relating a story he had fabricated, purposely to ruin me with her.

He began with observing to her that I was grown very handsome, and that M. de Guise wished to marry me; that his uncles, too, were very desirous of such a match; and, if I should entertain a like passion for him, there would be danger of my discovering to him all she said to me; that she well knew the ambition of that house, and how ready they were, on all occasions, to circumvent ours. It would, therefore, be proper that she should not, for the future, communicate any matter of State to me, but, by degrees, withdraw her confidence.

I discovered the evil effects proceeding from this pernicious advice on the very same evening. I remarked an unwillingness on her part to speak to me before my brother; and, as soon as she entered into discourse with him, she commanded me to go to bed. This command she repeated two or three times. I quitted her closet, and left them together in conversation; but, as soon as he was gone, I returned and entreated her to let me know if I had been so unhappy as to have done anything, through ignorance, which had given her offence. She was at first inclined to dissemble with me; but at length she said to me thus: "Daughter, your brother is prudent and cautious; you ought not to be displeased with him for what he does, and you must believe what I shall tell you is right and proper." She then related the conversation she had with my brother, as I have just written it; and she then ordered me never to speak to her in my brother's presence.

These words were like so many daggers plunged into my breast. In my disgrace, I experienced as much grief as I had before joy on being received into her favour and confidence. I did not omit to say everything to convince her of my entire ignorance of what my brother had told her. I said it was a matter I had never heard mentioned before; and that, had I known it, I should certainly have made her immediately acquainted with it. All I said was to no purpose; my brother's words had made the first impression; they were constantly present in her mind, and outweighed probability and truth. When I discovered this, I told her that I felt less uneasiness at being deprived of my happiness than I did joy when I had acquired it; for my brother had taken it from me, as he had given it. He had given it without reason; he had taken it away without cause. He had praised me for discretion and prudence when I did not merit it, and he suspected my fidelity on grounds wholly imaginary and fictitious. I concluded with assuring her that I should never forget my brother's behaviour on this occasion.

Hereupon she flew into a passion and commanded me not to make the least show of resentment at his behaviour. From that hour she gradually withdrew her favour from me. Her son became the god of her idolatry, at the shrine of whose will she sacrificed everything.

The grief which I inwardly felt was very great and overpowered all my faculties, until it wrought so far on my constitution as to contribute to my receiving the infection which then prevailed in the army. A few days after I fell sick of a raging fever, attended with purple spots, a malady which carried off numbers, and, amongst the rest, the two principal physicians belonging to the King and Queen, Chappelain and Castelan. Indeed, few got over the disorder after being attacked with it.

In this extremity the Queen my mother, who partly guessed the cause of my illness, omitted nothing that might serve to remove it; and, without fear of consequences, visited me frequently. Her goodness contributed much to my recovery; but my brother's hypocrisy was sufficient to destroy all the benefit I received from her attention, after having been guilty of so treacherous a proceeding. After he had proved so ungrateful to me, he came and sat at the foot of my bed from morning to night, and appeared as anxiously attentive as if we had been the most perfect friends. My mouth was shut up by the command I had received from the Queen our mother, so that I only answered his dissembled concern with sighs, like Burrus in the presence of Nero, when he was dying by the poison administered by the hands of that tyrant. The sighs, however, which I vented in my brother's presence, might convince him that I attributed my sickness rather to his ill offices than to the prevailing contagion.

God had mercy on me, and supported me through this dangerous illness. After I had kept my bed a fortnight, the army changed its quarters, and I was conveyed away with it in a litter. At the end of each day's march, I found King Charles at the door of my quarters, ready, with the rest of the good gentlemen belonging to the Court, to carry my litter up to my bedside. In this manner I came to Angers from St. Jean d'Angely, sick in body, but more sick in mind. Here, to my misfortune, M. de Guise and his uncles had arrived before me. This was a circumstance which gave my good brother great pleasure, as it afforded a colourable appearance to his story. I soon discovered the advantage my brother would make of it to increase my already too great mortification; for he came daily to see me, and as constantly brought M. de Guise into my chamber with him. He pretended the sincerest regard for De Guise, and, to make him believe it, would take frequent opportunities of embracing him, crying out at the same time, "would to God you were my brother!" This he often put in practice before me, which M. de Guise seemed not to comprehend; but I, who knew his malicious designs, lost all patience, yet did not dare to reproach him with his hypocrisy.

As soon as I was recovered, a treaty was set on foot for a marriage betwixt the King of Portugal and me, an ambassador having been sent for that purpose. The Queen my mother commanded me to prepare to give the ambassador an audience; which I did accordingly. My brother had made her believe that I was averse to this marriage; accordingly, she took me to task upon it, and questioned me on the subject, expecting she should find some cause to be angry with me. I told her my will had always been guided by her own, and that whatever she thought right for me to do, I should do it. She answered me, angrily, according as she had been wrought upon, that I did not speak the sentiments of my heart, for she well knew that the Cardinal de Lorraine had persuaded me into a promise of having his nephew. I begged her to forward this match with the King of Portugal, and I would convince her of my obedience to her commands. Every day some new matter was reported to incense her against me. All these were machinations worked up by the mind of Le Guast. In short, I was constantly receiving some fresh mortification, so that I hardly passed a day in quiet. On one side, the King of Spain was using his utmost endeavours to break off the match with Portugal, and M. de Guise, continuing at Court, furnished grounds for persecuting me on the other. Still, not a single person of the Guises ever mentioned a word to me on the subject; and it was well known that, for more than a twelvemonth, M. de Guise had been paying his addresses to the Princesse de Porcian; but the slow progress made in bringing this match to a conclusion was said to be owing to his designs upon me.

As soon as I made this discovery I resolved to write to my sister, Madame de Lorraine, who had a great influence in the House of Porcian, begging her to use her endeavours to withdraw M. de Guise from Court, and make him conclude his match with the Princess, laying open to her the plot which had been concerted to ruin the Guises and me. She readily saw through it, came immediately to Court, and concluded the match, which delivered me from the aspersions cast on my character, and convinced the Queen my mother that what I had told her was the real truth. This at the same time stopped the mouths of my enemies and gave me some repose.

At length the King of Spain, unwilling that the King of Portugal should marry out of his family, broke off the treaty which had been entered upon for my marriage with him.

# LETTER IV.

*Death of the Queen of Navarre—Marguerite's Marriage with Her Son, the King of Navarre, Afterwards Henri IV. of France.—The Preparations for That Solemnisation Described.—The Circumstances Which Led to the Massacre of the Huguenots on St. Bartholomew's Day.*

Some short time after this a marriage was projected betwixt the Prince of Navarre, now our renowned King Henri IV., and me.

The Queen my mother, as she sat at table, discoursed for a long time upon the subject with M. de Meru, the House of Montmorency having first proposed the match. After the Queen had risen from table, he told me she had commanded him to mention it to me. I replied that it was quite unnecessary, as I had no will but her own; however, I should wish she would be pleased to remember that I was a Catholic, and that I should dislike to marry any one of a contrary persuasion.

Soon after this the Queen sent for me to attend her in her closet. She there informed me that the Montmorencys had proposed this match to her, and that she was desirous to learn my sentiments upon it.

I answered that my choice was governed by her pleasure, and that I only begged her not to forget that I was a good Catholic.

This treaty was in negotiation for some time after this conversation, and was not finally settled until the arrival of the Queen of Navarre, his mother, at Court, where she died soon after.

Whilst the Queen of Navarre lay on her death-bed, a circumstance happened of
so whimsical a nature that, though not of consequence to merit a place in the history, it may very well deserve to be related by me to you. Madame de Nevers,
whose oddities you well know, attended the Cardinal de Bourbon, Madame de
Guise, the Princesse de Conde, her sisters, and myself to the late Queen of
Navarre's apartments, whither we all went to pay those last duties which her rank
and our nearness of blood demanded of us. We found the Queen in bed with her
curtains undrawn, the chamber not disposed with the pomp and ceremonies of
our religion, but after the simple manner of the Huguenots; that is to say, there
were no priests, no cross, nor any holy water. We kept ourselves at some distance
from the bed, but Madame de Nevers, whom you know the Queen hated more
than any woman besides, and which she had shown both in speech and by
actions, —Madame de Nevers, I say, approached the bedside, and, to the great
astonishment of all present, who well knew the enmity subsisting betwixt them,
took the Queen's hand, with many low curtseys, and kissed it; after which, making another curtsey to the very ground, she retired and rejoined us.

A few months after the Queen's death, the Prince of Navarre, or rather, as he was
then styled, the King, came to Paris in deep mourning, attended by eight hundred gentlemen, all in mourning habits. He was received with every honour by
King Charles and the whole Court, and, in a few days after his arrival, our marriage was solemnised with all possible magnificence; the King of Navarre and his
retinue putting off their mourning and dressing themselves in the most costly
manner. The whole Court, too, was richly attired; all which you can better conceive than I am able to express. For my own part, I was set out in a most royal
manner; I wore a crown on my head with the 'coet', or regal close gown of ermine,
and I blazed in diamonds. My blue-coloured robe had a train to it of four ells in
length, which was supported by three princesses. A platform had been raised,
some height from the ground, which led from the Bishop's palace to the Church
of Notre-Dame. It was hung with cloth of gold; and below it stood the people in
throngs to view the procession, stifling with heat. We were received at the church
door by the Cardinal de Bourbon, who officiated for that day, and pronounced
the nuptial benediction. After this we proceeded on the same platform to the trib-
une which separates the nave from the choir, where was a double staircase, one
leading into the choir, the other through the nave to the church door. The King
of Navarre passed by the latter and went out of church. But fortune, which is ever
changing, did not fail soon to disturb the felicity of this union. This was occasioned by the wound received by the Admiral, which had wrought the Huguenots
up to a degree of desperation. The Queen my mother was reproached on that
account in such terms by the elder Pardaillan and some other principal
Huguenots, that she began to apprehend some evil design. M. de Guise and my

brother the King of Poland, since Henri III. of France, gave it as their advice to be beforehand with the Huguenots. King Charles was of a contrary opinion. He had a great esteem for M. de La Rochefoucauld, Teligny, La Noue, and some other leading men of the same religion; and, as I have since heard him say, it was with the greatest difficulty he could be prevailed upon to give his consent, and not before he had been made to understand that his own life aid the safety of his kingdom depended upon it.

The King having learned that Maurevel had made an attempt upon the Admiral's life, by firing a pistol at him through a window,—in which attempt he failed, having wounded the Admiral only in the shoulder,—and supposing that Maurevel had done this at the instance of M. de Guise, to revenge the death of his father, whom the Admiral had caused to be killed in the same manner by Poltrot, he was so much incensed against M. de Guise that he declared with an oath that he would make an example of him; and, indeed, the King would have put M. de Guise under an arrest, if he had not kept out of his sight the whole day. The Queen my mother used every argument to convince King Charles that what had been done was for the good of the State; and this because, as I observed before, the King had so great a regard for the Admiral, La Noue, and Teligny, on account of their bravery, being himself a prince of a gallant and noble spirit, and esteeming others in whom he found a similar disposition. Moreover, these designing men had insinuated themselves into the King's favour by proposing an expedition to Flanders, with a view of extending his dominions and aggrandising his power, knew would secure to themselves an influence over his royal and generous mind.

Upon this occasion, the Queen my mother represented to the King that the attempt of M. de Guise upon the Admiral's life was excusable in a son who, being denied justice, had no other means of avenging his father's death. Moreover, the Admiral, she said, had deprived her by assassination, during his minority and her regency, of a faithful servant in the person of Charri, commander of the King's body-guard, which rendered him deserving of the like treatment.

Notwithstanding that the Queen my mother spoke thus to the King, discovering by her expressions and in her looks all the grief which she inwardly felt on the recollection of the loss of persons who had been useful to her; yet, so much was King Charles inclined to save those who, as he thought, would one day be serviceable to him, that he still persisted in his determination to punish M. de Guise, for whom he ordered strict search to be made.

At length Pardaillan, disclosing by his menaces, during the supper of the Queen my mother, the evil intentions of the Huguenots, she plainly perceived that things were brought to so near a crisis, that, unless steps were taken that very night to prevent it, the King and herself were in danger of being assassinated. She, therefore, came to the resolution of declaring to King Charles his real situation. For this purpose she thought of the Marechal de Rais as the most proper person to break the matter to the King, the Marshal being greatly in his favour and confidence.

Accordingly, the Marshal went to the King in his closet, between the hours of nine and ten, and told him he was come as a faithful servant to discharge his duty, and lay before him the danger in which he stood, if he persisted in his resolution of punishing M. de Guise, as he ought now to be informed that the attempt made upon the Admiral's life was not set on foot by him alone, but that his (the King's) brother the King of Poland, and the Queen his mother, had their shares in it; that he must be sensible how much the Queen lamented Charri's assassination, for which she had great reason, having very few servants about her upon whom she could rely, and as it happened during the King's minority,—at the time, moreover, when France was divided between the Catholics and the Huguenots, M. de Guise being at the head of the former, and the Prince de Conde of the latter, both alike striving to deprive him of his crown; that through Providence, both his crown and kingdom had been preserved by the prudence and good conduct of the Queen Regent, who in this extremity found herself powerfully aided by the said Charri, for which reason she had vowed to avenge his death; that, as to the Admiral, he must be ever considered as dangerous to the State, and whatever show he might make of affection for his Majesty's person, and zeal for his service in Flanders, they must be considered as mere pretences, which he used to cover his real design of reducing the kingdom to a state of confusion.

The Marshal concluded with observing that the original intention had been to make away with the Admiral only, as the most obnoxious man in the kingdom; but Maurevel having been so unfortunate as to fail in his attempt, and the Huguenots becoming desperate enough to resolve to take up arms, with design to attack, not only M. de Guise, but the Queen his mother, and his brother the King of Poland, supposing them, as well as his Majesty, to have commanded Maurevel to make his attempt, he saw nothing but cause of alarm for his Majesty's safety,— as well on the part of the Catholics, if he persisted in his resolution to punish M. de Guise, as of the Huguenots, for the reasons which he had just laid before him.

## LETTER V.

*The Massacre of St. Bartholomew's Day.*

King Charles, a prince of great prudence, always paying a particular deference to his mother, and being much attached to the Catholic religion, now convinced of the intentions of the Huguenots, adopted a sudden resolution of following his mother's counsel, and putting himself under the safeguard of the Catholics. It was not, however, without extreme regret that he found he had it not in his power to save Teligny, La Noue, and M. de La Rochefoucauld.

He went to the apartments of the Queen his mother, and sending for M. de Guise and all the Princes and Catholic officers, the "Massacre of St. Bartholomew" was that night resolved upon.

Immediately every hand was at work; chains were drawn across the streets, the alarm-bells were sounded, and every man repaired to his post, according to the orders he had received, whether it was to attack the Admiral's quarters, or those of the other Huguenots. M. de Guise hastened to the Admiral's, and Besme, a gentleman in the service of the former, a German by birth, forced into his chamber, and having slain him with a dagger, threw his body out of a window to his master.

I was perfectly ignorant of what was going forward. I observed every one to be in motion: the Huguenots, driven to despair by the attack upon the Admiral's life, and the Guises, fearing they should not have justice done them, whispering all they met in the ear.

The Huguenots were suspicious of me because I was a Catholic, and the Catholics because I was married to the King of Navarre, who was a Huguenot. This being the case, no one spoke a syllable of the matter to me.

At night, when I went into the bedchamber of the Queen my mother, I placed myself on a coffer, next my sister Lorraine, who, I could not but remark, appeared greatly cast down. The Queen my mother was in conversation with some one, but, as soon as she espied me, she bade me go to bed. As I was taking leave, my sister seized me by the hand and stopped me, at the same time shedding a flood of tears: "For the love of God," cried she, "do not stir out of this chamber!" I was greatly alarmed at this exclamation; perceiving which, the Queen my mother called my sister to her, and chid her very severely. My sister replied it was sending me away to be sacrificed; for, if any discovery should be made, I should be the first victim of their revenge. The Queen my mother made answer that, if it pleased God, I should receive no hurt, but it was necessary I should go, to prevent the suspicion that might arise from my staying.

I perceived there was something on foot which I was not to know, but what it was I could not make out from anything they said.

The Queen again bade me go to bed in a peremptory tone. My sister wished me a good night, her tears flowing apace, but she did not dare to say a word more; and I left the bedchamber more dead than alive.

As soon as I reached my own closet, I threw myself upon my knees and prayed to God to take me into his protection and save me; but from whom or what, I was ignorant. Hereupon the King my husband, who was already in bed, sent for me. I went to him, and found the bed surrounded by thirty or forty Huguenots, who were entirely unknown to me; for I had been then but a very short time married. Their whole discourse, during the night, was upon what had happened to the Admiral, and they all came to a resolution of the next day demanding justice of the King against M. de Guise; and, if it was refused, to take it themselves.

For my part, I was unable to sleep a wink the whole night, for thinking of my sister's tears and distress, which had greatly alarmed me, although I had not the least knowledge of the real cause. As soon as day broke, the King my husband said he would rise and play at tennis until King Charles was risen, when he would go to him immediately and demand justice. He left the bedchamber, and all his gentlemen followed.

As soon as I beheld it was broad day, I apprehended all the danger my sister had spoken of was over; and being inclined to sleep, I bade my nurse make the door fast, and I applied myself to take some repose. In about an hour I was awakened by a violent noise at the door, made with both hands and feet, and a voice calling out, "Navarre! Navarre!" My nurse, supposing the King my husband to be at the door, hastened to open it, when a gentleman, named M. de Teian, ran in, and threw himself immediately upon my bed. He had received a wound in his arm from a sword, and another by a pike, and was then pursued by four archers, who followed him into the bedchamber. Perceiving these last, I jumped out of bed, and the poor gentleman after me, holding me fast by the waist. I did not then know him; neither was I sure that he came to do me no harm, or whether the archers were in pursuit of him or me. In this situation I screamed aloud, and he cried out likewise, for our fright was mutual. At length, by God's providence, M. de Nangay, captain of the guard, came into the bed-chamber, and, seeing me thus surrounded, though he could not help pitying me, he was scarcely able to refrain from laughter. However, he reprimanded the archers very severely for their indiscretion, and drove them out of the chamber. At my request he granted the poor gentleman his life, and I had him put to bed in my closet, caused his wounds to be dressed, and did not suffer him to quit my apartment until he was perfectly cured. I changed my shift, because it was stained with the blood of this man, and, whilst I was doing so, De Nangay gave me an account of the transactions of the foregoing night, assuring me that the King my husband was safe, and actually at that moment in the King's bedchamber. He made me muffle myself up in a cloak, and conducted me to the apartment of my sister, Madame de Lorraine, whither I arrived more than half dead. As we passed through the antechamber, all the doors of which were wide open, a gentleman of the name of Bourse, pursued by archers, was run through the body with a pike, and fell dead at my feet. As if I had been killed by the same stroke, I fell, and was caught by M. de Nangay before I reached the ground. As soon as I recovered from this fainting-fit, I went into my sister's bedchamber, and was immediately followed by M. de Mioflano, first gentleman to the King my husband, and Armagnac, his first valet de chambre, who both came to beg me to save their lives. I went and threw myself on my knees before the King and the Queen my mother, and obtained the lives of both of them.

Five or six days afterwards, those who were engaged in this plot, considering that it was incomplete whilst the King my husband and the Prince de Conde remained alive, as their design was not only to dispose of the Huguenots, but of the Princes of the blood likewise; and knowing that no attempt could be made on my husband whilst I continued to be his wife, devised a scheme which they suggested to the Queen my mother for divorcing me from him. Accordingly, one holiday, when I waited upon her to chapel, she charged me to declare to her, upon my oath, whether I believed my husband to be like other men. "Because," said she, "if he is not, I can easily procure you a divorce from him." I begged her to believe that I was not sufficiently competent to answer such a question, and could only reply, as the Roman lady did to her husband, when he chid her for not informing him of his stinking breath, that, never having approached any other man near enough to know a difference, she thought all men had been alike in that respect. "But," said I, "Madame, since you have put the question to me, I can only declare I am content to remain as I am;" and this I said because I suspected the design of separating me from my husband was in order to work some mischief against him.

# LETTER VI.

*Henri, Duc d'Anjou, Elected King of Poland, Leaves France.— Huguenot Plots to Withdraw the Duc d'Alencon and the King of Navarre from Court.—Discovered and Defeated by Marguerite's Vigilance.—She Draws Up an Eloquent Defence, Which Her Husband Delivers before a Committee from the Court of Parliament.—Alencon and Her Husband, under a Close Arrest, Regain Their Liberty by the Death of Charles IX.*

We accompanied the King of Poland as far as Beaumont. For some months before he quitted France, he had used every endeavour to efface from my mind the ill offices he had so ungratefully done me. He solicited to obtain the same place in my esteem which he held during our infancy; and, on taking leave of me, made me confirm it by oaths and promises. His departure from France, and King Charles's sickness, which happened just about the same time, excited the spirit of the two factions into which the kingdom was divided, to form a variety of plots. The Huguenots, on the death of the Admiral, had obtained from the King my husband, and my brother Alencon, a written obligation to avenge it. Before St. Bartholomew's Day, they had gained my brother over to their party, by the hope of securing Flanders for him. They now persuaded my husband and him to leave the King and Queen on their return, and pass into Champagne, there to join some troops which were in waiting to receive them.

M. de Miossans, a Catholic gentleman, having received an intimation of this design, considered it so prejudicial to the interests of the King his master, that he communicated it to me with the intention of frustrating a plot of so much danger to themselves, and to the State. I went immediately to the King and the Queen my mother, and informed them that. I had a matter of the utmost importance to lay before them; but that I could not declare it unless they would be pleased to promise me that no harm should ensue from it to such as I should name to them, and that they would put a stop to what was going forward without publishing their knowledge of it. Having obtained my request, I told them that my brother Alencon and the King my husband had an intention, on the very next day, of joining some Huguenot troops, which expected them, in order to fulfil the engagement they had made upon the Admiral's death; and for this their intention, I begged they might be excused, and that they might be prevented from going away without any discovery being made that their designs had been found out. All this was granted me, and measures were so prudently taken to stay them, that they had not the least suspicion that their intended evasion was known. Soon after, we arrived at St. Germain, where we stayed some time, on account of the King's indisposition. All this while my brother Alencon used every means he could devise to ingratiate himself with me, until at last I promised him my friendship, as I had before done to my brother the King of Poland. As he had been brought up at a distance from Court, we had hitherto known very little of each other, and kept ourselves at a distance. Now that he had made the first advances, in so respectful and affectionate a manner, I resolved to receive him into a firm friendship, and to interest myself in whatever concerned him, without prejudice, however, to the interests of my good brother King Charles, whom I loved more than any one besides, and who continued to entertain a great regard for me, of which he gave me proofs as long as he lived.

Meanwhile King Charles was daily growing worse, and the Huguenots constantly forming new plots. They were very desirous to get my brother the Duc d'Alencon and the King my husband away from Court. I got intelligence, from time to time, of their designs; and, providentially, the Queen my mother defeated their intentions when a day had been fixed on for the arrival of the Huguenot troops at St. Germain.

To avoid this visit, we set off the night before for Paris, two hours after midnight, putting King Charles in a litter, and the Queen my mother taking my brother and the King my husband with her in her own carriage.

They did not experience on this occasion such mild treatment as they had hitherto done, for the King going to the Wood of Vincennes, they were not permitted to set foot out of the palace. This misunderstanding was so far from being mitigated by time, that the mistrust and discontent were continually increasing, owing to the insinuations and bad advice offered to the King by those who wished the ruin and downfall of our house. To such a height had these jealousies risen that the Marechaux de Montmorency and de Cosse were put under a close arrest, and La Mole and the Comte de Donas executed. Matters were now arrived at such a pitch that commissioners were appointed from the Court of Parliament to hear and determine upon the case of my brother and the King my husband.

My husband, having no counsellor to assist him, desired me to draw up his defence in such a manner that he might not implicate any person, and, at the same time, clear my brother and himself from any criminality of conduct. With God's help I accomplished this task to his great satisfaction, and to the surprise of the commissioners, who did not expect to find them so well prepared to justify themselves.

As it was apprehended, after the death of La Mole and the Comte de Donas, that their lives were likewise in danger, I had resolved to save them at the hazard of my own ruin with the King, whose favour I entirely enjoyed at that time. I was suffered to pass to and from them in my coach, with my women, who were not even required by the guard to unmask, nor was my coach ever searched. This being the case, I had intended to convey away one of them disguised in a female habit. But the difficulty lay in settling betwixt themselves which should remain behind in prison, they being closely watched by their guards, and the escape of one bringing the other's life into hazard. Thus they could never agree upon the point, each of them wishing to be the person I should deliver from confinement.

But Providence put a period to their imprisonment by a means which proved very unfortunate for me. This was no other than the death of King Charles, who was the only stay and support of my life,—a brother from whose hands I never received anything but good; who, during the persecution I underwent at Angers, through my brother Anjou, assisted me with all his advice and credit. In a word, when I lost King Charles, I lost everything.

## LETTER VII.

*Accession of Henri III.—A Journey to Lyons.—Marguerite's Faith in Supernatural Intelligence.*

After this fatal event, which was as unfortunate for France as for me, we went to Lyons to give the meeting to the King of Poland, now Henri III. of France. The new King was as much governed by Le Guast as ever, and had left this intriguing, mischievous man behind in France to keep his party together. Through this man's insinuations he had conceived the most confirmed jealousy of my brother Alencon. He suspected that I was the bond that connected the King my husband and my brother, and that, to dissolve their union, it would be necessary to create a coolness between me and my husband, and to work up a quarrel of rivalship betwixt them both by means of Madame de Sauves, whom they both visited. This abominable plot, which proved the source of so much disquietude and unhappiness, as well to my brother as myself, was as artfully conducted as it was wickedly designed.

Many have held that God has great personages more immediately under his protection, and that minds of superior excellence have bestowed on them a good genius, or secret intelligencer, to apprise them of good, or warn them against evil. Of this number I might reckon the Queen my mother, who has had frequent intimations of the kind; particularly the very night before the tournament which proved so fatal to the King my father, she dreamed that she saw him wounded in the eye, as it really happened; upon which she awoke, and begged him not to run a course that day, but content himself with looking on. Fate prevented the nation from enjoying so much happiness as it would have done had he followed her advice. Whenever she lost a child, she beheld a bright flame shining before her, and would immediately cry out, "God save my children!" well knowing it was the harbinger of the death of some one of them, which melancholy news was sure to be confirmed very shortly after. During her very dangerous illness at Metz, where she caught a pestilential fever, either from the coal fires, or by visiting some of the nunneries which had been infected, and from which she was restored to health and to the kingdom through the great skill and experience of that modern Asculapius, M. de Castilian, her physician—I say, during that illness, her bed being surrounded by my brother King Charles, my brother and sister Lorraine, several members of the Council, besides many ladies and princesses, not choosing to quit her, though without hopes of her life, she was heard to cry out, as if she saw the battle of Jarnac: "There! see how they flee! My son, follow them to victory! Ah, my son falls! O my God, save him! See there! the Prince de Conde is dead!" All who were present looked upon these words as proceeding from her delirium, as she knew that my brother Anjou was on the point of giving battle, and thought no more of it. On the night following, M. de Losses brought the news of the battle; and, it being supposed that she would be pleased to hear of it, she was awakened, at which she appeared to be angry, saying: "Did I not know it yesterday?" It was then that those about her recollected what I have now related, and concluded that it was no delirium, but one of those revelations made by God to great and illustrious persons. Ancient history furnishes many examples of the like kind amongst the pagans, as the apparition of Brutus and many others, which I shall not mention, it not being my intention to illustrate these Memoirs with such narratives, but only to relate the truth, and that with as much expedition as I am able, that you may be the sooner in possession of my story.

I am far from supposing that I am worthy of these divine admonitions; nevertheless, I should accuse myself of ingratitude towards my God for the benefits I have received, which I esteem myself obliged to acknowledge whilst I live; and I further believe myself bound to bear testimony of his goodness and power, and the mercies he hath shown me, so that I can declare no extraordinary accident ever befell me, whether fortunate or otherwise, but I received some warning of it, either by dream or in some other way, so that I may say with the poet

> "De mon bien, on mon mal,
> Mon esprit m'est oracle."

> (Whate'er of good or ill befell,
> My mind was oracle to tell.)

And of this I had a convincing proof on the arrival of the King of Poland, when the Queen my mother went to meet him. Amidst the embraces and compliments of welcome in that warm season, crowded as we were together and stifling with heat, I found a universal shivering come over me, which was plainly perceived by those near me. It was with difficulty I could conceal what I felt when the King, having saluted the Queen my mother, came forward to salute me. This secret intimation of what was to happen thereafter made a strong impression on my mind at the moment, and I thought of it shortly after, when I discovered that the King had conceived a hatred of me through the malicious suggestions of Le Guast, who had made him believe, since the King's death, that I espoused my brother Alencon's party during his absence, and cemented a friendship betwixt the King my husband and him.

# LETTER VIII.

*What Happened at Lyons.*

An opportunity was diligently sought by my enemies to effect their design of bringing about a misunderstanding betwixt my brother Alencon, the King my husband, and me, by creating a jealousy of me in my husband, and in my brother and husband, on account of their mutual love for Madame de Sauves.

One afternoon, the Queen my mother having retired to her closet to finish some despatches which were likely to detain her there for some time, Madame de Nevers, your kinswoman, Madame de Rais, another of your relations, Bourdeille, and Surgeres asked me whether I would not wish to see a little of the city. Whereupon Mademoiselle de Montigny, the niece of Madame Usez, observing to us that the Abbey of St. Pierre was a beautiful convent, we all resolved to visit it. She then begged to go with us, as she said she had an aunt in that convent, and as it was not easy to gain admission into it, except in the company of persons of distinction. Accordingly, she went with us; and there being six of us, the carriage was crowded. Over and above those I have mentioned, there was Madame de Curton, the lady of my bedchamber, who always attended me. Liancourt, first esquire to the King, and Camille placed themselves on the steps of Torigni's carriage, supporting themselves as well as they were able, making themselves merry on the occasion, and saying they would go and see the handsome nuns, too. I look upon it as ordered by Divine Providence that I should have Mademoiselle de Montigny with me, who was not well acquainted with any lady of the company, and that the two gentlemen just mentioned, who were in the confidence of King Henri, should likewise be of the party, as they were able to clear me of the calumny intended to be fixed upon me.

Whilst we were viewing the convent, my carriage waited for us in the square. In the square many gentlemen belonging to the Court had their lodgings. My carriage was easily to be distinguished, as it was gilt and lined with yellow velvet trimmed with silver. We had not come out of the convent when the King passed through the square on his way to see Quelus, who was then sick. He had with him the King my husband, D'O———— , and the fat fellow Ruff.

The King, observing no one in my carriage, turned to my husband and said: "There is your wife's coach, and that is the house where Bide lodges. Bide is sick, and I will engage my word she is gone upon a visit to him. Go," said he to Ruff, "and see whether she is not there." In saying this, the King addressed himself to a proper tool for his malicious purpose, for this fellow Ruffs was entirely devoted to Le Guast. I need not tell you he did not find me there; however, knowing the King's intention, he, to favour it, said loud enough for the King my husband to hear him: "The birds have been there, but they are now flown." This furnished sufficient matter for conversation until they reached home.

Upon this occasion, the King my husband displayed all the good sense and generosity of temper for which he is remarkable. He saw through the design, and he despised the maliciousness of it. The King my brother was anxious to see the Queen my mother before me, to whom he imparted the pretended discovery, and she, whether to please a son on whom she doted, or whether she really gave credit to the story, had related it to some ladies with much seeming anger.

Soon afterwards I returned with the ladies who had accompanied me to St. Pierre's, entirely ignorant of what had happened. I found the King my husband in our apartments, who began to laugh on seeing me, and said: "Go immediately to the Queen your mother, but I promise you you will not return very well pleased." I asked him the reason, and what had happened. He answered: "I shall tell you nothing; but be assured of this, that I do not give the least credit to the story, which I plainly perceive to be fabricated in order to stir up a difference betwixt us two, and break off the friendly intercourse between your brother and me."

Finding I could get no further information on the subject from him, I went to the apartment of the Queen my mother. I met M. de Guise in the antechamber, who was not displeased at the prospect of a dissension in our family, hoping that he might make some advantage of it. He addressed me in these words: "I waited here expecting to see you, in order to inform you that some ill office has been done you with the Queen." He then told me the story he had learned of D'O————, who, being intimate with your kinswoman, had informed M. de Guise of it, that he might apprise us.

I went into the Queen's bedchamber, but did not find my mother there. However, I saw Madame de Nemours, the rest of the princesses, and other ladies, who all exclaimed on seeing me: "Good God! the Queen your mother is in such a rage; we would advise you, for the present, to keep out of her sight."

"Yes," said I, "so I would, had I been guilty of what the King has reported; but I assure you all I am entirely innocent, and must therefore speak with her and clear myself."

I then went into her closet, which was separated from the bedchamber by a slight partition only, so that our whole conversation could be distinctly heard. She no sooner set eyes upon me than she flew into a great passion, and said everything that the fury of her resentment suggested. I related to her the whole truth, and begged to refer her to the company which attended me, to the number of ten or twelve persons, desiring her not to rely on the testimony of those more immediately about me, but examine Mademoiselle Montigny, who did not belong to me, and Liancourt and Camille, who were the King's servants.

She would not hear a word I had to offer, but continued to rate me in a furious manner; whether it was through fear, or affection for her son, or whether she believed the story in earnest, I know not. When I observed to her that I understood the King had done me this ill office in her opinion, her anger was redoubled, and she endeavoured to make me believe that she had been informed of the circumstance by one of her own valets de chambre, who had himself seen me at the place. Perceiving that I gave no credit to this account of the matter, she became more and more incensed against me.

All that was said was perfectly heard by those in the next room. At length I left her closet, much chagrined; and returning to my own apartments, I found the King my husband there, who said to me:

"Well, was it not as I told you?"

He, seeing me under great concern, desired me not to grieve about it, adding that "Liancourt and Camille would attend the King that night in his bedchamber, and relate the affair as it really was; and to-morrow," continued he, "the Queen your mother will receive you in a very different manner."

"But, monsieur," I replied, "I have received too gross an affront in public to forgive those who were the occasion of it; but that is nothing when compared with the malicious intention of causing so heavy a misfortune to befall me as to create a variance betwixt you and me."

"But," said he, "God be thanked, they have failed in it."

"For that," answered I, "I am the more beholden to God and your amiable disposition. However," continued I, "we may derive this good from it, that it ought to be a warning to us to put ourselves upon our guard against the King's stratagems to bring about a disunion betwixt you and my brother, by causing a rupture betwixt you and me."

Whilst I was saying this, my brother entered the apartment, and I made them renew their protestations of friendship. But what oaths or promises can prevail against love! This will appear more fully in the sequel of my story.

An Italian banker, who had concerns with my brother, came to him the next morning, and invited him, the King my husband, myself, the princesses, and other ladies, to partake of an entertainment in a garden belonging to him. Having made it a constant rule, before and after I married, as long as I remained in the Court of the Queen my mother, to go to no place without her permission, I waited on her, at her return from mass, and asked leave to be present at this banquet. She refused to give any leave, and said she did not care where I went. I leave you to judge, who know my temper, whether I was not greatly mortified at this rebuff.

Whilst we were enjoying this entertainment, the King, having spoken with Liancourt, Camille, and Mademoiselle Montigny, was apprised of the mistake which the malice or misapprehension of Ruff had led him into. Accordingly, he went to the Queen my mother and related the whole truth, entreating her to remove any ill impressions that might remain with me, as he perceived that I was not deficient in point of understanding, and feared that I might be induced to engage in some plan of revenge.

When I returned from the banquet before mentioned, I found that what the King my husband had foretold was come to pass; for the Queen my mother sent for me into her back closet, which was adjoining the King's, and told me that she was now acquainted with the truth, and found I had not deceived her with a false story. She had discovered, she said, that there was not the least foundation for the report her valet de chambre had made, and should dismiss him from her service as a bad man. As she perceived by my looks that I saw through this disguise, she said everything she could think of to persuade me to a belief that the King had not mentioned it to her. She continued her arguments, and I still appeared incredulous. At length the King entered the closet, and made many apologies, declaring he had been imposed on, and assuring me of his most cordial friendship and esteem; and thus matters were set to rights again.

## LETTER IX.

*Fresh Intrigues.—Marriage of Henri III.—Bussi Arrives at Court and Narrowly Escapes Assassination.*

After staying some time at Lyons, we went to Avignon. Le Guast, not daring to hazard any fresh imposture, and finding that my conduct afforded no ground for jealousy on the part of my husband, plainly perceived that he could not, by that means, bring about a misunderstanding betwixt my brother and the King my husband. He therefore resolved to try what he could effect through Madame de Sauves. In order to do this, he obtained such an influence over her that she acted entirely as he directed; insomuch that, by his artful instructions, the passion which these young men had conceived, hitherto wavering and cold, as is generally the case at their time of life, became of a sudden so violent that ambition and every obligation of duty were at once absorbed by their attentions to this woman.

This occasioned such a jealousy betwixt them that, though her favours were divided with M. de Guise, Le Guast, De Souvray, and others, any one of whom she preferred to the brothers-in-law, such was the infatuation of these last, that each considered the other as his only rival.

To carry on De Guast's sinister designs, this woman persuaded the King my husband that I was jealous of her, and on that account it was that I joined with my brother. As we are ready to give ear and credit to those we love, he believed all she said. From this time he became distant and reserved towards me, shunning my presence as much as possible; whereas, before, he was open and communicative to me as to a sister, well knowing that I yielded to his pleasure in all things, and was far from harbouring jealousy of any kind.

What I had dreaded, I now perceived had come to pass. This was the loss of his favour and good opinion; to preserve which I had studied to gain his confidence by a ready compliance with his wishes, well knowing that mistrust is the sure forerunner of hatred.

I now turned my mind to an endeavour to wean my brother's affection from Madame de Sauves, in order to counterplot Le Guast in his design to bring about a division, and thereby to effect our ruin. I used every means with my brother to divert his passion; but the fascination was too strong, and my pains proved ineffectual. In anything else, my brother would have suffered himself to be ruled by me; but the charms of this Circe, aided by that sorcerer, Le Guast, were too powerful to be dissolved by my advice. So far was he from profiting by my counsel that he was weak enough to communicate it to her. So blind are lovers!

Her vengeance was excited by this communication, and she now entered more fully into the designs of Le Guast. In consequence, she used all her art to, make the King my husband conceive an aversion for me; insomuch that he scarcely ever spoke with me. He left her late at night, and, to prevent our meeting in the morning, she directed him to come to her at the Queen's levee, which she duly attended; after which he passed the rest of the day with her. My brother likewise followed her with the greatest assiduity, and she had the artifice to make each of them think that he alone had any place in her esteem. Thus was a jealousy kept up betwixt them, and, in consequence, disunion and mutual ruin.

We made a considerable stay at Avignon, whence we proceeded through Burgundy and Champagne to Rheims, where the King's marriage was celebrated. From Rheims we came to Paris, things going on in their usual train, and Le Guast prosecuting his designs, with all the success he could wish. At Paris my brother was joined by Bussi, whom he received with all the favour which his bravery merited. He was inseparable from my brother, in consequence of which I frequently saw him, for my brother and I were always together, his household being equally at my devotion as if it were my own. Your aunt, remarking this harmony betwixt us, has often told me that it called to her recollection the times of my uncle, M. d'Orleans, and my aunt, Madame de Savoie.

Le Guast thought this a favourable circumstance to complete his design. Accordingly, he suggested to Madame de Sauves to make my husband believe that it was on account of Bussi that I frequented my brother's apartments so constantly.

The King my husband, being fully informed of all my proceedings from persons in his service who attended me everywhere, could not be induced to lend an ear to this story. Le Guast, finding himself foiled in this quarter, applied to the King, who was well inclined to listen to the tale, on account of his dislike to my brother and me, whose friendship for each other was unpleasing to him.

Besides this, he was incensed against Bussi, who, being formerly attached to him, had now devoted himself wholly to my brother,—an acquisition which, on account of the celebrity of Bussi's fame for parts and valour, redounded greatly to my brother's honour, whilst it increased the malice and envy of his enemies.

The King, thus worked upon by Le Guast, mentioned it to the Queen my mother, thinking it would have the same effect on her as the tale which was trumped up at Lyons. But she, seeing through the whole design, showed him the improbability of the story, adding that he must have some wicked people about him, who could put such notions in his head, observing that I was very unfortunate to have fallen upon such evil times. "In my younger days," said she, "we were allowed to converse freely with all the gentlemen who belonged to the King our father, the Dauphin, and M. d'Orléans, your uncles. It was common for them to assemble in the bedchamber of Madame Marguerite, your aunt, as well as in mine, and nothing was thought of it. Neither ought it to appear strange that Bussi sees my daughter in the presence of her husband's servants. They are not shut up together. Bussi is a person of quality, and holds the first place in your brother's family. What grounds are there for such a calumny? At Lyons you caused me to offer her an affront, which I fear she will never forget."

The King was astonished to hear his mother talk in this manner, and interrupted her with saying:

"Madame, I only relate what I have heard."

"But who is it," answered she, "that tells you all this? I fear no one that intends you any good, but rather one that wishes to create divisions amongst you all."

As soon as the King had left her she told me all that had passed, and said: "You are unfortunate to live in these times." Then calling your aunt, Madame de Dampierre, they entered into a discourse concerning the pleasures and innocent freedoms of the times they had seen, when scandal and malevolence were unknown at Court.

Le Guast, finding this plot miscarry, was not long in contriving another. He addressed himself for this purpose to certain gentlemen who attended the King my husband. These had been formerly the friends of Bussi, but, envying the glory he had obtained, were now become his enemies. Under the mask of zeal for their master, they disguised the envy, which they harboured in their breasts. They entered into a design of assassinating Bussi as he left my brother to go to his own lodgings, which was generally at a late hour. They knew that he was always accompanied home by fifteen or sixteen gentlemen, belonging to my brother, and that, notwithstanding he wore no sword, having been lately wounded in the right arm, his presence was sufficient to inspire the rest with courage.

In order, therefore, to make sure work, they resolved on attacking him with two or three hundred men, thinking that night would throw a veil over the disgrace of such an assassination.

Le Guast, who commanded a regiment of guards, furnished the requisite number of men, whom he disposed in five or six divisions, in the street through which he was to pass. Their orders were to put out the torches and flambeaux, and then to fire their pieces, after which they were to charge his company, observing particularly to attack one who had his right arm slung in a scarf.

Fortunately they escaped the intended massacre, and, fighting their way through, reached Bussi's lodgings, one gentleman only being killed, who was particularly attached to M. de Bussi, and who was probably mistaken for him, as he had his arm likewise slung in a scarf.

An Italian gentleman, who belonged to my brother, left them at the beginning of the attack, and came running back to the Louvre. As soon as he reached my brother's chamber door, he cried out aloud:

"Busai is assassinated!" My brother was going out, but I, hearing the cry of assassination, left my chamber, by good fortune not being undressed, and stopped my brother. I then sent for the Queen my mother to come with all haste in order to prevent him from going out, as he was resolved to do, regardless of what might happen. It was with difficulty we could stay him, though the Queen my mother represented the hazard he ran from the darkness of the night, and his ignorance of the nature of the attack, which might have been purposely designed by Le Guast to take away his life. Her entreaties and persuasions would have been of little avail if she had not used her authority to order all the doors to be barred, and taken the resolution of remaining where she was until she had learned what had really happened.

Bussi, whom God had thus miraculously preserved, with that presence of mind which he was so remarkable for in time of battle and the most imminent danger, considering within himself when he reached home the anxiety of his master's mind should he have received any false report, and fearing he might expose himself to hazard upon the first alarm being given (which certainly would have been the case, if my mother had not interfered and prevented it), immediately despatched one of his people to let him know every circumstance.

The next day Busai showed himself at the Louvre without the least dread of enemies, as if what had happened had been merely the attack of a tournament. My brother exhibited much pleasure at the sight of Busai, but expressed great resentment at such a daring attempt to deprive him of so brave and valuable a servant, a man whom Le Guast durst not attack in any other way than by a base assassination.

## LETTER X.

*Bussi Is Sent from Court.—Marguerite's Husband Attacked with a Fit of Epilepsy.— Her Great Care of Him.—Torigni Dismissed from Marguerite's Service.—The King of Navarre and the Duc d'Alencon Secretly Leave the Court.*

The Queen my mother, a woman endowed with the greatest prudence and fore-sight of any one I ever knew, apprehensive of evil consequences from this affair, and fearing a dissension betwixt her two sons, advised my brother to fall upon some pretence for sending Bussi away from Court. In this advice I joined her, and, through our united counsel and request, my brother was prevailed upon to give his consent. I had every reason to suppose that Le Guast would take advantage of the rencounter to foment the coolness which already existed betwixt my brother and the King my husband into an open rupture. Bussi, who implicitly followed my brother's directions in everything, departed with a company of the bravest noblemen that were about the latter's person.

Bussi was now removed from the machinations of Le Guast, who likewise failed in accomplishing a design he had long projected,—to disunite the King my husband and me.

One night my husband was attacked with a fit, and continued insensible for the space of an hour,—occasioned, I supposed, by his excesses with women, for I never knew anything of the kind to happen to him before. However, as it was my duty so to do, I attended him with so much care and assiduity that, when he recovered, he spoke of it to every one, declaring that, if I had not perceived his indisposition and called for the help of my women, he should not have survived the fit.

From this time he treated me with more kindness, and the cordiality betwixt my brother and him was again revived, as if I had been the point of union at which they were to meet, or the cement that joined them together.

Le Guast was now at his wit's end for some fresh contrivance to breed disunion in the Court.

He had lately persuaded the King to remove from about the person of the Queen-consort a princess of the greatest virtue and most amiable qualities, a female attendant of the name of Changi, for whom the Queen entertained a particular esteem, as having been brought up with her. Being successful in this measure, he now thought of making the King my husband send away Torigni, whom I greatly regarded.

The argument he used with the King was, that young princesses ought to have no favourites about them.

The King, yielding to this man's persuasions, spoke of it to my husband, who observed that it would be a matter that would greatly distress me; that if I had an esteem for Torigni it was not without cause, as she had been brought up with the Queen of Spain and me from our infancy; that, moreover, Torigni was a young lady of good understanding, and had been of great use to him during his confinement at Vincennes; that it would be the greatest ingratitude in him to overlook services of such a nature, and that he remembered well when his Majesty had expressed the same sentiments.

Thus did he defend himself against the performance of so ungrateful an action. However, the King listened only to the arguments of Le Guast, and told my husband that he should have no more love for him if he did not remove Torigni from about me the very next morning.

He was forced to comply, greatly contrary to his will, and, as he has since declared to me, with much regret. Joining entreaties to commands, he laid his injunctions on me accordingly.

How displeasing this separation was I plainly discovered by the many tears I shed on receiving his orders. It was in vain to represent to him the injury done to my character by the sudden removal of one who had been with me from my earliest years, and was so greatly, in my esteem and confidence; he could not give an ear to my reasons, being firmly bound by the promise he had made to the King.

Accordingly, Torigni left me that very day, and went to the house of a relation, M. Chastelas. I was so greatly offended with this fresh indignity, after so many of the kind formerly received, that I could not help yielding to resentment; and my grief and concern getting the upper hand of my prudence, I exhibited a great coolness and indifference towards my husband. Le Guast and Madame de Sauves were successful in creating a like indifference on his part, which, coinciding with mine, separated us altogether, and we neither spoke to each other nor slept in the same bed.

A few days after this, some faithful servants about the person of the King my husband remarked to him the plot which had been concerted with so much artifice to lead him to his ruin, by creating a division, first betwixt him and my brother, and next betwixt him and me, thereby separating him from those in whom only he could hope for his principal support. They observed to him that already matters were brought to such a pass that the King showed little regard for him, and even appeared to despise him.

They afterwards addressed themselves to my brother, whose situation was not in the least mended since the departure of Bussi, Le Guast causing fresh indignities to be offered him daily. They represented to him that the King my husband and he were both circumstanced alike, and equally in disgrace, as Le Guast had everything under his direction; so that both of them were under the necessity of soliciting, through him, any favours which they might want of the King, and which, when demanded, were constantly refused them with great contempt. Moreover, it was become dangerous to offer them service, as it was inevitable ruin for any one to do so.

"Since, then," said they, "your dissensions appear to be so likely to prove fatal to both, it would be advisable in you both to unite and come to a determination of leaving the Court; and, after collecting together your friends and servants, to require from the King an establishment suitable to your ranks." They observed to my brother that he had never yet been put in possession of his appanage, and received for his subsistence only some certain allowances, which were not regularly paid him, as they passed through the hands of Le Guast, and were at his disposal, to be discharged or kept back, as he judged proper. They concluded with observing that, with regard to the King my husband, the government of Guyenne was taken out of his hands; neither was he permitted to visit that or any other of his dominions.

It was hereupon resolved to pursue the counsel now given, and that the King my husband and my brother should immediately withdraw themselves from Court.

My brother made me acquainted with this resolution, observing to me, as my husband and he were now friends again, that I ought to forget all that had passed; that my husband had declared to him that he was sorry things had so happened, that we had been outwitted by our enemies, but that he was resolved, from henceforward, to show me every attention and give me every proof of his love and esteem, and he concluded with begging me to make my husband every show of affection, and to be watchful for their interest during their absence.

It was concerted betwixt them that my brother should depart first, making off in a carriage in the best manner he could; that, in a few days afterwards, the King my husband should follow, under pretence of going on a hunting party. They both expressed their concern that they could not take me with them, assuring me that I had no occasion to have any apprehensions, as it would soon appear that they had no design to disturb the peace of the kingdom, but merely to ensure the safety of their own persons, and to settle their establishments. In short, it might well be supposed that, in their present situation, they had danger to themselves from such reason to apprehend as had evil designs against their family.

Accordingly, as soon as it was dusk, and before the King's supper-time, my brother changed his cloak, and concealing the lower part of his face to his nose in it, left the palace, attended by a servant who was little known, and went on foot to the gate of St. Honore, where he found Simier waiting for him in a coach, borrowed of a lady for the purpose.

My brother threw himself into it, and went to a house about a quarter of a league out of Paris, where horses were stationed ready; and at the distance of about a league farther, he joined a party of two or three hundred horsemen of his servants, who were awaiting his coming. My brother was not missed till nine o'clock, when the King and the Queen my mother asked me the reason he did not come to sup with them as usual, and if I knew of his being indisposed. I told them I had not seen him since noon. Thereupon they sent to his apartments. Word was brought back that he was not there. Orders were then given to inquire at the apartments of the ladies whom he was accustomed to visit. He was nowhere to be found. There was now a general alarm. The King flew into a great passion, and began to threaten me. He then sent for all the Princes and the great officers of the Court; and giving orders for a pursuit to be made, and to bring him back, dead or alive, cried out:

"He is gone to make war against me; but I will show him what it is to contend with a king of my power."

Many of the Princes and officers of State remonstrated against these orders, which they observed ought to be well weighed. They said that, as their duty directed, they were willing to venture their lives in the King's service; but to act against his brother they were certain would not be pleasing to the King himself; that they were well convinced his brother would undertake nothing that should give his Majesty displeasure, or be productive of danger to the realm; that perhaps his leaving the Court was owing to some disgust, which it would be more advisable to send and inquire into. Others, on the contrary, were for putting the King's orders into execution; but, whatever expedition they could use, it was day before they set off; and as it was then too late to overtake my brother, they returned, being only equipped for the pursuit.

I was in tears the whole night of my brother's departure, and the next day was seized with a violent cold, which was succeeded by a fever that confined me to my bed.

Meanwhile my husband was preparing for his departure, which took up all the time he could spare from his visits to Madame de Sauves; so that he did not think of me. He returned as usual at two or three in the morning, and, as we had separate beds, I seldom heard him; and in the morning, before I was awake, he went to my mother's levee, where he met Madame de Sauves, as usual.

This being the case, he quite forgot his promise to my brother of speaking to me; and when he went, away, it was without taking leave of me.

The King did not show my husband more favour after my brother's evasion, but continued to behave with his former coolness. This the more confirmed him in the resolution of leaving the Court, so that in a few days, under the pretence of hunting, he went away.

# LETTER XI.

*Queen Marguerite under Arrest.—Attempt on Torigni's Life.—Her Fortunate Deliverance.*

The King, supposing that I was a principal instrument in aiding the Princes in their desertion, was greatly incensed against me, and his rage became at length so violent that, had not the Queen my mother moderated it, I am inclined to think my life had been in danger. Giving way to her counsel, he became more calm, but insisted upon a guard being placed over me, that I might not follow the King my husband, neither have communication with any one, so as to give the Princes intelligence of what was going on at Court. The Queen my mother gave her consent to this measure, as being the least violent, and was well pleased to find his anger cooled in so great a degree. She, however, requested that she might be permitted to discourse with me, in order to reconcile me to a submission to treatment of so different a kind from what I had hitherto known. At the same time she advised the King to consider that these troubles might not be lasting; that everything in the world bore a double aspect; that what now appeared to him horrible and alarming, might, upon a second view, assume a more pleasing and tranquil look; that, as things changed, so should measures change with them; that there might come a time when he might have occasion for my services; that, as prudence counselled us not to repose too much confidence in our friends, lest they should one day become our enemies, so was it advisable to conduct ourselves in such a manner to our enemies as if we had hopes they should hereafter become our friends. By such prudent remonstrances did the Queen my mother restrain the King from proceeding to extremities with me, as he would otherwise possibly have done.

Le Guast now endeavoured to divert his fury to another object, in order to wound me in a most sensitive part. He prevailed on the King to adopt a design for seizing Torigni, at the house of her cousin Chastelas, and, under pretence of bringing her before the King, to drown her in a river which they were to cross. The party sent upon this errand was admitted by Chastelas, not suspecting any evil design, without the least difficulty, into his house. As soon as they had gained admission they proceeded to execute the cruel business they were sent upon, by fastening Torigni with cords and locking her up in a chamber, whilst their horses were baiting. Meantime, according to the French custom, they crammed themselves, like gluttons, with the best eatables the house afforded.

Chastelas, who was a man of discretion, was not displeased to gain time at the expense of some part of his substance, considering that the suspension of a sentence is a prolongation of life, and that during this respite the King's heart might relent, and he might countermand his former orders. With these considerations he was induced to submit, though it was in his power to have called for assistance to repel this violence. But God, who hath constantly regarded my afflictions and afforded me protection against the malicious designs of my enemies, was pleased to order poor Torigni to be delivered by means which I could never have devised had I been acquainted with the plot, of which I was totally ignorant. Several of the domestics, male as well as female, had left the house in a fright, fearing the insolence and rude treatment of this troop of soldiers, who behaved as riotously as if they were in a house given up to pillage. Some of these, at the distance of a quarter of a league from the house, by God's providence, fell in with Ferte and Avantigni, at the head of their troops, in number about two hundred horse, on their march to join my brother. Ferte, remarking a labourer, whom he knew to belong to Chastelas, apparently in great distress, inquired of him what was the matter, and whether he had been ill-used by any of the soldiery. The man related to him all he knew, and in what state he had left his master's house. Hereupon Ferte and Avantigni resolved, out of regard to me, to effect Torigni's deliverance, returning thanks to God for having afforded them so favourable an opportunity of testifying the respect they had always entertained towards me.

Accordingly, they proceeded to the house with all expedition, and arrived just at the moment these soldiers were setting Torigni on horseback, for the purpose of conveying her to the river wherein they had orders to plunge her. Galloping into the courtyard, sword in hand, they cried out: "Assassins, if you dare to offer that lady the least injury, you are dead men!" So saying, they attacked them and drove them to flight, leaving their prisoner behind, nearly as dead with joy as she was before with fear and apprehension. After returning thanks to God and her deliverers for so opportune and unexpected a rescue, she and her cousin Chastelas set off in a carriage, under the escort of their rescuers, and joined my brother, who, since he could not have me with him, was happy to have one so dear to me about him. She remained under my brother's protection as long as any danger was apprehended, and was treated with as much respect as if she had been with me.

Whilst the King was giving directions for this notable expedition, for the purpose of sacrificing Torigni to his vengeance, the Queen my mother, who had not received the least intimation of it, came to my apartment as I was dressing to go abroad, in order to observe how I should be received after what had passed at Court, having still some alarms on account of my husband and brother. I had hitherto confined myself to my chamber, not having perfectly recovered my health, and, in reality, being all the time as much indisposed in mind as in body.

My mother, perceiving my intention, addressed me in these words: "My child, you are giving yourself unnecessary trouble in dressing to go abroad. Do not be alarmed at what I am going to tell you. Your own good sense will dictate to you that you ought not to be surprised if the King resents the conduct of your brother and husband, and as he knows the love and friendship that exist between you three, should suppose that you were privy to their design of leaving the Court. He has, for this reason, resolved to detain you in it, as a hostage for them. He is sensible how much you are beloved by your husband, and thinks he can hold no pledge that is more dear to him. On this account it is that the King has ordered his guards to be placed, with directions not to suffer you to leave your apartments. He has done this with the advice of his counsellors, by whom it was suggested that, if you had your free liberty, you might be induced to advise your brother and husband of their deliberations. I beg you will not be offended with these measures, which, if it so please God, may not be of long continuance. I beg, moreover, you will not be displeased with me if I do not pay you frequent visits, as I should be unwilling to create any suspicions in the King's mind. However, you may rest assured that I shall prevent any further steps from being taken that may prove disagreeable to you, and that I shall use my utmost endeavours to bring about a reconciliation betwixt your brothers."

I represented to her, in reply, the great indignity that was offered to me by putting me under arrest; that it was true my brother had all along communicated to me the just cause he had to be dissatisfied, but that, with respect to the King my husband, from the time Torigni was taken from me we had not spoken to each other; neither had he visited me during my indisposition, nor did he even take leave of me when he left Court. "This," says she, "is nothing at all; it is merely a trifling difference betwixt man and wife, which a few sweet words, conveyed in a letter, will set to rights. When, by such means, he has regained your affections, he has only to write to you to come to him, and you will set off at the very first opportunity. Now, this is what the King my son wishes to prevent."

# LETTER XII.

*The Peace of Sens betwixt Henri III. and the Huguenots.*

The Queen my mother left me, saying these words. For my part, I remained a close prisoner, without a visit from a single person, none of my most intimate friends daring to come near me, through the apprehension that such a step might prove injurious to their interests. Thus it is ever in Courts. Adversity is solitary, while prosperity dwells in a crowd; the object of persecution being sure to be shunned by his nearest friends and dearest connections. The brave Grillon was the only one who ventured to visit me, at the hazard of incurring disgrace. He came five or six times to see me, and my guards were so much astonished at his resolution, and awed by his presence, that not a single Cerberus of them all would venture to refuse him entrance to my apartments.

Meanwhile, the King my husband reached the States under his government. Being joined there by his friends and dependents, they all represented to him the indignity offered to me by his quitting the Court without taking leave of me. They observed to him that I was a princess of good understanding, and that it would be for his interest to regain my esteem; that, when matters were put on their former footing, he might derive to himself great advantage from my presence at Court. Now that he was at a distance from his Circe, Madame de Sauves, he could listen to good advice. Absence having abated the force of her charms, his eyes were opened; he discovered the plots and machinations of our enemies, and clearly perceived that a rupture could not but tend to the ruin of us both.

Accordingly, he wrote me a very affectionate letter, wherein he entreated me to forget all that had passed betwixt us, assuring me that from thenceforth he would ever love me, and would give me every demonstration that he did so, desiring me to inform him of what was going on at Court, and how it fared with me and my brother. My brother was in Champagne and the King my husband in Gascony, and there had been no communication betwixt them, though they were on terms of friendship.

I received this letter during my imprisonment, and it gave me great comfort under that situation. Although my guards had strict orders not to permit me to set pen to paper, yet, as necessity is said to be the mother of invention, I found means to write many letters to him. Some few days after I had been put under arrest, my brother had intelligence of it, which chagrined him so much that, had not the love of his country prevailed with him, the effects of his resentment would have been shown in a cruel civil war, to which purpose he had a sufficient force entirely at his devotion. He was, however, withheld by his patriotism, and contented himself with writing to the Queen my mother, informing her that, if I was thus treated, he should be driven upon some desperate measure. She, fearing the consequence of an open rupture, and dreading lest, if blows were once struck, she should be deprived of the power of bringing about a reconciliation betwixt the brothers, represented the consequences to the King, and found him well disposed to lend an ear to her reasons, as his anger was now cooled by the apprehensions of being attacked in Gascony, Dauphiny, Languedoc, and Poitou, with all the strength of the Huguenots under the King my husband. Besides the many strong places held by the Huguenots, my brother had an army with him in Champagne, composed chiefly of nobility, the bravest and best in France. The King found, since my brother's departure, that he could not, either by threats or rewards, induce a single person among the princes and great lords to act against him, so much did every one fear to intermeddle in this quarrel, which they considered as of a family nature; and after having maturely reflected on his situation, he acquiesced in my mother's opinion, and begged her to fall upon some means of reconciliation. She thereupon proposed going to my brother and taking me with her. To the measure of taking me, the King had an objection, as he considered me as the hostage for my husband and brother. She then agreed to leave me behind, and set off without my knowledge of the matter. At their interview, my brother represented to the Queen my mother that he could not but be greatly dissatisfied with the King after the many mortifications he had received at Court; that the cruelty and injustice of confining me hurt him equally as if done to himself; observing, moreover, that, as if my arrest were not a sufficient mortification, poor Torigni must be made to suffer; and concluding with the declaration of his firm resolution not to listen to any terms of peace until I was restored to my liberty, and reparation made me for the indignity I had sustained. The Queen my mother being unable to obtain any other answer, returned to Court and acquainted the King with my brother's determination. Her advice was to go back again with me, for going without me, she said, would answer very little purpose; and if I went with her in disgust, it would do more harm than good. Besides, there was reason to fear, in that case, I should insist upon going to my husband. "In short," says she, "my daughter's guard must be removed, and she must be satisfied in the best way we can."

The King agreed to follow her advice, and was now, on a sudden, as eager to reconcile matters betwixt us as she was herself. Hereupon I was sent for, and when I came to her, she informed me that she had paved the way for peace; that it was for the good of the State, which she was sensible I must be as desirous to promote as my brother; that she had it now in her power to make a peace which would be as satisfactory as my brother could desire, and would put us entirely out of the reach of Le Guast's machinations, or those of any one else who might have an influence over the King's mind. She observed that, by assisting her to procure a good understanding betwixt the King and my brother, I should relieve her from that cruel disquietude under which she at present laboured, as, should things come to an open rupture, she could not but be grieved, whichever party prevailed, as they were both her sons. She therefore expressed her hopes that I would forget the injuries I had received, and dispose myself to concur in a peace, rather than join in any plan of revenge. She assured me that the King was sorry for what had happened; that he had even expressed his regret to her with tears in his eyes, and had declared that he was ready to give me every satisfaction. I replied that I was willing to sacrifice everything for the good of my brothers and of the State; that I wished for nothing so much as peace, and that I would exert myself to the utmost to bring it about.

As I uttered these words, the King came into the closet, and, with a number of fine speeches, endeavoured to soften my resentment and to recover my friendship, to which I made such returns as might show him I harboured no ill-will for the injuries I had received. I was induced to such behaviour rather out of contempt, and because it was good policy to let the King go away satisfied with me.

Besides, I had found a secret pleasure, during my confinement, from the perusal of good books, to which I had given myself up with a delight I never before experienced. I consider this as an obligation I owe to fortune, or, rather, to Divine Providence, in order to prepare me, by such efficacious means, to bear up against the misfortunes and calamities that awaited me. By tracing nature in the universal book which is opened to all mankind, I was led to the knowledge of the Divine

Author. Science conducts us, step by step, through the whole range of creation, until we arrive, at length, at God. Misfortune prompts us to summon our utmost strength to oppose grief and recover tranquillity, until at length we find a powerful aid in the knowledge and love of God, whilst prosperity hurries us away until we are overwhelmed by our passions. My captivity and its consequent solitude afforded me the double advantage of exciting a passion for study, and an inclination for devotion, advantages I had never experienced during the vanities and splendour of my prosperity.

As I have already observed, the King, discovering in me no signs of discontent, informed me that the Queen my mother was going into Champagne to have an interview with my brother, in order to bring about a peace, and begged me to accompany her thither and to use my best endeavours to forward his views, as he knew my brother was always well disposed to follow my counsel; and he concluded with saying that the peace, when accomplished, he should ever consider as being due to my good offices, and should esteem himself obliged to me for it. I promised to exert myself in so good a work, which I plainly perceived was both for my brother's advantage and the benefit of the State.

The Queen my mother and I set off for Sens the next day. The conference was agreed to be held in a gentleman's chateau, at a distance of about a league from that place. My brother was waiting for us, accompanied by a small body of troops and the principal Catholic noblemen and princes of his army. Amongst these were the Duc Casimir and Colonel Poux, who had brought him six thousand German horse, raised by the Huguenots, they having joined my brother, as the King my husband and he acted in conjunction.

The treaty was continued for several days, the conditions of peace requiring much discussion, especially such articles of it as related to religion. With respect to these, when at length agreed upon, they were too much to the advantage of the Huguenots, as it appeared afterwards, to be kept; but the Queen my mother gave in to them, in order to have a peace, and that the German cavalry before mentioned might be disbanded. She was, moreover, desirous to get my brother out of the hands of the Huguenots; and he was himself as willing to leave them, being always a very good Catholic, and joining the Huguenots only through necessity. One condition of the peace was, that my brother should have a suitable establishment. My brother likewise stipulated for me, that my marriage portion should be assigned in lands, and M. de Beauvais, a commissioner on his part, insisted much upon it. My mother, however, opposed it, and persuaded me to join her in it, assuring me that I should obtain from the King all I could require. Thereupon I begged I might not be included in the articles of peace, observing that I would rather owe whatever I was to receive to the particular favour of the King and the Queen my mother, and should, besides, consider it as more secure when obtained by such means.

The peace being thus concluded and ratified on both sides, the Queen my mother prepared to return. At this instant I received letters from the King my husband, in which he expressed a great desire to see me, begging me, as soon as peace was agreed on, to ask leave to go to him. I communicated my husband's wish to the Queen my mother, and added my own entreaties. She expressed herself greatly averse to such a measure, and used every argument to set me against it. She observed that, when I refused her proposal of a divorce after St. Bartholomew's Day, she gave way to my refusal, and commended me for it, because my husband was then converted to the Catholic religion; but now that he had abjured Catholicism, and was turned Huguenot again, she could not give her consent that I should go to him. When I still insisted upon going, she burst into a flood of tears, and said, if I did not return with her, it would prove her ruin; that the King would believe it was her doing; that she had promised to bring me back with her; and that, when my brother returned to Court, which would be soon, she would give her consent.

We now returned to Paris, and found the King well satisfied that we had made a peace; though not, however, pleased with the articles concluded in favour of the Huguenots. He therefore resolved within himself, as soon as my brother should return to Court, to find some pretext for renewing the war. These advantageous conditions were, indeed, only granted the Huguenots to get my brother out of their hands, who was detained near two months, being employed in disbanding his German horse and the rest of his army.

# LETTER XIII.

*The League.—War Declared against the Huguenots.— Queen Marguerite Sets out for Spa.*

At length my brother returned to Court, accompanied by all the Catholic nobility who had followed his fortunes. The King received him very graciously, and showed, by his reception of him, how much he was pleased at his return. Bussi, who returned with my brother, met likewise with a gracious reception. Le Guast was now no more, having died under the operation of a particular regimen ordered for him by his physician. He had given himself up to every kind of debauchery; and his death seemed the judgment of the Almighty on one whose body had long been perishing, and whose soul had been made over to the prince of demons as the price of assistance through the means of diabolical magic, which he constantly practised. The King, though now without this instrument of his malicious contrivances, turned his thoughts entirely upon the destruction of the Huguenots. To effect this, he strove to engage my brother against them, and thereby make them his enemies and that I might be considered as another enemy, he used every means to prevent me from going to the King my husband. Accordingly he showed every mark of attention to both of us, and manifested an inclination to gratify all our wishes.

After some time, M. de Duras arrived at Court, sent by the King my husband to hasten my departure. Hereupon, I pressed the King greatly to think well of it, and give me his leave. He, to colour his refusal, told me he could not part with me at present, as I was the chief ornament of his Court; that he must, keep me a little longer, after which he would accompany me himself on my way as far as Poitiers.

With this answer and assurance, he sent M. de Duras back. These excuses were purposely framed in order to gain time until everything was prepared for declaring war against the Huguenots, and, in consequence, against the King my husband, as he fully designed to do.

As a pretence to break with the Huguenots, a report was spread abroad that the Catholics were dissatisfied with the Peace of Sens, and thought the terms of it too advantageous for the Huguenots. This rumour succeeded, and produced all that discontent amongst the Catholics intended by it. A league was formed: in the provinces and great cities, which was joined by numbers of the Catholics. M. de Guise was named as the head of all. This was well known to the King, who pretended to be ignorant of what was going forward, though nothing else was talked of at Court.

The States were convened to meet at Blois. Previous to the opening of this assembly, the King called my brother to his closet, where were present the Queen my mother and some of the King's counsellors. He represented the great consequence the Catholic league was to his State and authority, even though they should appoint De Guise as the head of it; that such a measure was of the highest importance to them both, meaning my brother and himself; that the Catholics had very just reason to be dissatisfied with the peace, and that it behoved him, addressing himself to my brother, rather to join the Catholics than the Huguenots, and this from conscience as well as interest. He concluded his address to my brother with conjuring him, as a son of France and a good Catholic, to assist him with his aid and counsel in this critical juncture, when his crown and the Catholic religion were both at stake. He further said that, in order to get the start of so formidable a league, he ought to form one himself, and become the head of it, as well to show his zeal for religion as to prevent the Catholics from uniting under any other leader. He then proposed to declare himself the head of a league, which should be joined by my brother, the princes, nobles, governors, and others holding offices under the Government. Thus was my brother reduced to the necessity of making his Majesty a tender of his services for the support and maintenance of the Catholic religion.

The King, having now obtained assurances of my brother's assistance in the event of a war, which was his sole view in the league which he had formed with so much art, assembled together the princes and chief noblemen of his Court, and, calling for the roll of the league, signed it first himself, next calling upon my brother to sign it, and, lastly, upon all present.

The next day the States opened their meeting, when the King, calling upon the Bishops of Lyons, Ambrune, Vienne, and other prelates there present, for their advice, was told that, after the oath taken at his coronation, no oath made to heretics could bind him, and therefore he was absolved from his engagements with the Huguenots.

This declaration being made at the opening of the assembly, and war declared against the Huguenots, the King abruptly dismissed from Court the Huguenot, Genisac, who had arrived a few days before, charged by the King my husband with a commission to hasten my departure. The King very sharply told him that his sister had been given to a Catholic, and not to a Huguenot; and that if the King my husband expected to have me, he must declare himself a Catholic.

Every preparation for war was made, and nothing else talked of at Court; and, to make my brother still more obnoxious to the Huguenots, he had the command of an army given him. Genisac came and informed me of the rough message he had been dismissed with. Hereupon I went directly to the closet of the Queen my mother, where I found the King. I expressed my resentment at being deceived by him, and at being cajoled by his promise to accompany me from Paris to Poitiers, which, as it now appeared, was a mere pretence. I represented that I did not marry by my own choice, but entirely agreeable to the advice of King Charles, the Queen my mother, and himself; that, since they had given him to me for a husband, they ought not to hinder me from partaking of his fortunes; that I was resolved to go to him, and that if I had not their leave, I would get away how I could, even at the hazard of my life. The King answered: "Sister, it is not now a time to importune me for leave. I acknowledge that I have, as you say, hitherto prevented you from going, in order to forbid it altogether. From the time the King of Navarre changed his religion, and again became a Huguenot, I have been against your going to him. What the Queen my mother and I are doing is for your good. I am determined to carry on a war of extermination until this wretched religion of the Huguenots, which is of so mischievous a nature, is no more. Consider, my sister, if you, who are a Catholic, were once in their hands, you would become a hostage for me, and prevent my design. And who knows but they might seek their revenge upon me by taking away your life? No, you shall not go amongst them; and if you leave us in the manner you have now mentioned, rely upon it that you will make the Queen your mother and me your bitterest enemies, and that we shall use every means to make you feel the effects of our resentment; and, moreover, you will make your husband's situation worse instead of better."

I went from this audience with much dissatisfaction, and, taking advice of the principal persons of both sexes belonging to Court whom I esteemed my friends, I found them all of opinion that it would be exceedingly improper for me to remain in a Court now at open variance with the King my husband. They recommended me not to stay at Court whilst the war lasted, saying it would be more honourable for me to leave the kingdom under the pretence of a pilgrimage, or a visit to some of my kindred. The Princesse de Roche-sur-Yon was amongst those I consulted upon the occasion, who was on the point of setting off for Spa to take the waters there.

My brother was likewise present at the consultation, and brought with him Mondoucet, who had been to Flanders in quality of the King's agent, whence he was just returned to represent to the King the discontent that had arisen amongst the Flemings on account of infringements made by the Spanish Government on the French laws. He stated that he was commissioned by several nobles, and the municipalities of several towns, to declare how much they were inclined in their hearts towards France, and how ready they were to come under a French government. Mondoucet, perceiving the King not inclined to listen to his representation, as having his mind wholly occupied by the war he had entered into with the Huguenots, whom he was resolved to punish for having joined my brother, had ceased to move in it further to the King, and addressed himself on the subject to my brother. My brother, with that princely spirit which led him to undertake great achievements, readily lent an ear to Mondoucet's proposition, and promised to engage in it, for he was born rather to conquer than to keep what he conquered. Mondoucet's proposition was the more pleasing to him as it was not unjust, it being, in fact, to recover to France what had been usurped by Spain.

Mondoucet had now engaged himself in my brother's service, and was to return to Flanders' under a pretence of accompanying the Princesse de Roche-sur-Yon in her journey to Spa; and as this agent perceived my counsellers to be at a loss for some pretence for my leaving Court and quitting France during the war, and that at first Savoy was proposed for my retreat, then Lorraine, and then Our Lady of Loretto, he suggested to my brother that I might be of great use to him in Flanders, if, under the colour of any complaint, I should be recommended to drink the Spa waters, and go with the Princesse de Roche-sur-Yon. My brother acquiesced in this opinion, and came up to me, saying: "Oh, Queen! you need be no longer at a loss for a place to go to. I have observed that you have frequently an erysipelas on your arm, and you must accompany the Princess to Spa. You must say, your physicians had ordered those waters for the complaint; but when they, did so, it was not the season to take them. That season is now approaching, and you hope to have the King's leave to go there."

My brother did not deliver all he wished to say at that time, because the Cardinal de Bourbon was present, whom he knew to be a friend to the Guises and to Spain. However, I saw through his real design, and that he wished me to promote his views in Flanders.

The company approved of my brother's advice, and the Princesse de Roche- sur-Yon heard the proposal with great joy, having a great regard for me. She promised to attend me to the Queen my mother when I should ask her consent.

The next day I found the Queen alone, and represented to her the extreme regret I experienced in finding that a war was inevitable betwixt the King my husband and his Majesty, and that I must continue in a state of separation from my husband; that, as long as the war lasted, it was neither decent nor honourable for me to stay at Court, where I must be in one or other, or both, of these cruel situations either that the King my husband should believe that I continued in it out of inclination, and think me deficient in the duty I owed him; or that his Majesty should entertain suspicions of my giving intelligence to the King my husband. Either of these cases, I observed, could not but prove injurious to me. I therefore prayed her not to take it amiss if I desired to remove myself from Court, and from becoming so unpleasantly situated; adding that my physicians had for some time recommended me to take the Spa waters for an erysipelas—to which I had been long subject—on my arm; the season for taking these waters was now approaching, and that if she approved of it, I would use the present opportunity, by which means I should be at a distance from Court, and show my husband that, as I could not be with him, I was unwilling to remain amongst his enemies. I further expressed my hopes that, through her prudence, a peace might be effected in a short time betwixt the King my husband and his Majesty, and that my husband might be restored to the favour he formerly enjoyed; that whenever I learned the news of so joyful an event, I would renew my solicitations to be permitted to go to my husband. In the meantime, I should hope for her permission to have the honour of accompanying the Princesse de Roche-sur- Yon, there present, in her journey to Spa.

She approved of what I proposed, and expressed her satisfaction that I had taken so prudent a resolution. She observed how much she was chagrined when she found that the King, through the evil persuasions of the bishops, had resolved to break through the conditions of the last peace, which she had concluded in his name. She saw already the ill effects of this hasty proceeding, as it had removed from the King's Council many of his ablest and best servants. This gave her, she said, much concern, as it did likewise to think I could not remain at Court without offending my husband, or creating jealousy and suspicion in the King's mind. This being certainly what was likely to be the consequence of my staying, she would advise the King to give me leave to set out on this journey.

She was as good as her word, and the King discoursed with me on the subject without exhibiting the smallest resentment. Indeed, he was well pleased now that he had prevented me from going to the King my husband, for whom he had conceived the greatest animosity.

He ordered a courier to be immediately despatched to Don John of Austria,—who commanded for the King of Spain in Flanders,—to obtain from him the necessary passports for a free passage in the countries under his command, as I should be obliged to cross a part of Flanders to reach Spa, which is in the bishopric of Liege.

All matters being thus arranged, we separated in a few days after this interview. The short time my brother and I remained together was employed by him in giving me instructions for the commission I had undertaken to execute for him in Flanders. The King and the Queen my mother set out for Poitiers, to be near the army of M. de Mayenne, then besieging Brouage, which place being reduced, it was intended to march into Gascony and attack the King my husband.

My brother had the command of another army, ordered to besiege Issoire and some other towns, which he soon after took.

For my part, I set out on my journey to Flanders accompanied by the Princesse de Roche-sur-Yon, Madame de Tournon, the lady of my bedchamber, Madame de Mouy of Picardy, Madame de Chastelaine, De Millon, Mademoiselle d'Atric, Mademoiselle de Tournon, and seven or eight other young ladies. My male attendants were the Cardinal de Lenoncourt, the Bishop of Langres, and M. de Mouy, Seigneur de Picardy, at present father-in-law to the brother of Queen Louise, called the Comte de Chalingy, with my principal steward of the household, my chief esquires, and the other gentlemen of my establishment.

# LETTER XIV.

*Description of Queen Marguerite's Equipage.—Her Journey to Liege Described.—She Enters with Success upon Her Mission.— Striking Instance of Maternal Duty and Affection in a Great Lady.— Disasters near the Close of the Journey.*

The cavalcade that attended me excited great curiosity as it passed through the several towns in the course of my journey, and reflected no small degree of cred-it on France, as it was splendidly set out, and made a handsome appearance. I travelled in a litter raised with pillars. The lining of it was Spanish velvet, of a crimson colour, embroidered in various devices with gold and different coloured silk thread.

The windows were of glass, painted in devices. The lining and windows had, in the whole, forty devices, all different and alluding to the sun and its effects. Each device had its motto, either in the Spanish or Italian language. My litter was fol-lowed by two others; in the one was the Princesse de Roche-sur-Yon, and in the other Madame de Tournon, my lady of the bedchamber. After them followed ten maids of honour, on horseback, with their governess; and, last of all, six coaches and chariots, with the rest of the ladies and all our female attendants.

I took the road of Picardy, the towns in which province had received the King's orders to pay me all due honours. Being arrived at Le Catelet, a strong place, about three leagues distant from the frontier of the Cambresis, the Bishop of Cambray (an ecclesiastical State acknowledging the King of Spain only as a guar-antee) sent a gentleman to inquire of me at what hour I should leave the place, as he intended to meet me on the borders of his territory.

Accordingly I found him there, attended by a number of his people, who appeared to be true Flemings, and to have all the rusticity and unpolished manners of their country. The Bishop was of the House of Barlemont, one of the principal families in Flanders. All of this house have shown themselves Spaniards at heart, and at that time were firmly attached to Don John. The Bishop received me with great politeness and not a little of the Spanish ceremony.

Although the city of Cambray is not so well built as some of our towns in France, I thought it, notwithstanding, far more pleasant than many of these, as the streets and squares are larger and better disposed. The churches are grand and highly ornamented, which is, indeed, common to France; but what I admired, above all, was the citadel, which is the finest and best constructed in Christendom.

The Spaniards experienced it to be strong whilst my brother had it in his possession. The governor of the citadel at this time was a worthy gentleman named M. d'Ainsi, who was, in every respect, a polite and well- accomplished man, having the carriage and behaviour of one of our most perfect courtiers, very different from the rude incivility which appears to be the characteristic of a Fleming.

The Bishop gave us a grand supper, and after supper a ball, to which he had invited all the ladies of the city. As soon as the ball was opened he withdrew, in accordance with the Spanish ceremony; but M. d'Ainsi did the honours for him, and kept me company during the ball, conducting me afterwards to a collation, which, considering his command at the citadel, was, I thought, imprudent. I speak from experience, having been taught, to my cost, and contrary to my desire, the caution and vigilance necessary to be observed in keeping such places. As my regard for my brother was always predominant in me, I continually had his instructions in mind, and now thought I had a fair opportunity to open my commission and forward his views in Flanders, this town of Cambray, and especially the citadel, being, as it were, a key to that country. Accordingly I employed all the talents God had given me to make M. d'Ainsi a friend to France, and attach him to my brother's interest. Through God's assistance I succeeded with him, and so much was M. d'Ainsi pleased with my conversation that he came to the resolution of soliciting the Bishop, his master, to grant him leave to accompany me as, far as Namur, where Don John of Austria was in waiting to receive me, observing that he had a great desire to witness so splendid an interview. This Spanish Fleming, the Bishop, had the weakness to grant M. d'Ainsi's request, who continued following in my train for ten or twelve days. During this time he took every opportunity of discoursing with me, and showed that, in his heart, he was well disposed to embrace the service of France, wishing no better master than the Prince my brother, and declaring that he heartily despised being under the command of his Bishop, who, though his sovereign, was not his superior by birth, being born a private gentleman like himself, and, in every other respect, greatly his inferior.

Leaving Cambray, I set out to sleep at Valenciennes, the chief city of a part of Flanders called by the same name. Where this country is divided from Cambresis (as far as which I was conducted by the Bishop of Cambray), the Comte de Lalain, M. de Montigny his brother, and a number of gentlemen, to the amount of two or three hundred, came to meet me.

Valenciennes is a town inferior to Cambray in point of strength, but equal to it for the beauty of its squares, and churches,—the former ornamented with fountains, as the latter are with curious clocks. The ingenuity of the Germans in the construction of their clocks was a matter of great surprise to all my attendants, few amongst whom had ever before seen clocks exhibiting a number of moving figures, and playing a variety of tunes in the most agreeable manner.

The Comte de Lalain, the governor of the city, invited the lords and gentlemen of my train to a banquet, reserving himself to give an entertainment to the ladies on our arrival at Mons, where we should find the Countess his wife, his sister-in-law Madame d'Aurec, and other ladies of distinction. Accordingly the Count, with his attendants, conducted us thither the next day. He claimed a relationship with the King my husband, and was, in reality, a person who carried great weight and authority. He was much dissatisfied with the Spanish Government, and had conceived a great dislike for it since the execution of Count Egmont, who was his near kinsman.

Although he had hitherto abstained from entering into the league with the Prince of Orange and the Huguenots, being himself a steady Catholic, yet he had not admitted of an interview with Don John, neither would he suffer him, nor any one in the interest of Spain, to enter upon his territories. Don John was unwilling to give the Count any umbrage, lest he should force him to unite the Catholic League of Flanders, called the League of the States, to that of the Prince of Orange and the Huguenots, well foreseeing that such a union would prove fatal to the Spanish interest, as other governors have since experienced. With this disposition of mind, the Comte de Lalain thought he could not give me sufficient demonstrations of the joy he felt by my presence; and he could not have shown more honour to his natural prince, nor displayed greater marks of zeal and affection.

On our arrival at Mons, I was lodged in his house, and found there the Countess his wife, and a Court consisting of eighty or a hundred ladies of the city and country. My reception was rather that of their sovereign lady than of a foreign princess. The Flemish ladies are naturally lively, affable, and engaging. The Comtesse de Lalain is remarkably so, and is, moreover, a woman of great sense and elevation of mind, in which particular, as well as in air and countenance, she carries a striking resemblance to the lady your cousin. We became immediately intimate, and commenced a firm friendship at our first meeting. When the supper hour came, we sat down to a banquet, which was succeeded by a ball; and this rule the Count observed as long as I stayed at Mons, which was, indeed, longer than I intended. It had been my intention to stay at Mons one night only, but the Count's obliging lady prevailed on me to pass a whole week there. I strove to excuse myself from so long a stay, imagining it might be inconvenient to them; but whatever I could say availed nothing with the Count and his lady, and I was under the necessity of remaining with them eight days. The Countess and I were on so familiar a footing that she stayed in my bedchamber till a late hour, and would not have left me then had she not imposed upon herself a task very rarely performed by persons of her rank, which, however, placed the goodness of her disposition in the most amiable light. In fact, she gave suck to her infant son; and one day at table, sitting next me, whose whole attention was absorbed in the promotion of my brother's interest,—the table being the place where, according to the custom of the country, all are familiar and ceremony is laid aside,—she, dressed out in the richest manner and blazing with diamonds, gave the breast to her child without rising from her seat, the infant being brought to the table as superbly habited as its nurse, the mother. She performed this maternal duty with so much good humour, and with a gracefulness peculiar to herself, that this charitable office— which would have appeared disgusting and been considered as an affront if done by some others of equal rank—gave pleasure to all who sat at table, and, accordingly, they signified their approbation by their applause.

The tables being removed, the dances commenced in the same room wherein we had supped, which was magnificent and large. The Countess and I sitting side by side, I expressed the pleasure I received from her conversation, and that I should place this meeting amongst the happiest events of my life. "Indeed," said I, "I shall have cause to regret that it ever did take place, as I shall depart hence so unwillingly, there being so little probability, of our meeting again soon. Why did Heaven deny, our being born in the same country!"

This was said in order to introduce my brother's business. She replied: "This country did, indeed, formerly belong to France, and our lawyers now plead their causes in the French language. The greater part of the people here still retain an affection for the French nation. For my part," added the Countess, "I have had a strong attachment to your country ever since I have had the honour of seeing you.

This country has been long in the possession of the House of Austria, but the regard of the people for that house has been greatly, weakened by the death of Count Egmont, M. de Horne, M. de Montigny, and others of the same party, some of them our near relations, and all of the best families of the country. We entertain the utmost dislike for the Spanish Government, and wish for nothing so much as to throw off the yoke of their tyranny; but, as the country is divided betwixt different religions, we are at a loss how to effect it if we could unite, we should soon drive out the Spaniards; but this division amongst ourselves renders us weak. Would to God the King your brother would come to a resolution of reconquering this country, to which he has an ancient claim! We should all receive him with open arms."

This was a frank declaration, made by the Countess without premeditation, but it had been long agitated in the minds of the people, who considered that it was from France they were to hope for redress from the evils with which they were afflicted. I now found I had as favourable an opening as I could wish for to declare my errand. I told her that the King of France my brother was averse to engaging in foreign war, and the more so as the Huguenots in his kingdom were too strong to admit of his sending any large force out of it. "My brother Alencon," said I, "has sufficient means, and might be induced to undertake it. He has equal valour, prudence, and benevolence with the King my brother or any of his ancestors. He has been bred to arms, and is esteemed one of the bravest generals of these times. He has the command of the King's army against the Huguenots, and has lately taken a well-fortified town, called Issoire, and some other places that were in their possession. You could not invite to your assistance a prince who has it so much in his power to give it; being not only a neighbour, but having a kingdom like France at his devotion, whence he may expect to derive the necessary aid and succour. The Count your husband may be assured that if he do my brother this good office he will not find him ungrateful, but may set what price he pleases upon his meritorious service. My brother is of a noble and generous disposition, and ready to requite those who do him favours. He is, moreover, an admirer of men of honour and gallantry, and accordingly is followed by the bravest and best men France has to boast of. I am in hopes that a peace will soon be reestablished with the Huguenots, and expect to find it so on my return to France. If the Count your husband think as you do, and will permit me to speak to him on the subject, I will engage to bring my brother over to the proposal, and, in that case, your country in general, and your house in particular, will be well satisfied with him. If, through your means, my brother should establish himself here, you may depend on seeing me often, there being no brother or sister who has a stronger affection for each other."

The Countess appeared to listen to what I said with great pleasure, and acknowledged that she had not entered upon this discourse without design. She observed
that, having perceived I did her the honour to have some regard for her, she had
resolved within herself not to let me depart out of the country without explain-
ing to me the situation of it, and begging me to procure the aid of France to
relieve them from the apprehensions of living in a state of perpetual war or of submitting to Spanish tyranny. She thereupon entreated me to allow her to relate our
present conversation to her husband, and permit them both to confer with me on
the subject the next day. To this I readily gave my consent.

Thus we passed the evening in discourse upon the object of my mission, and I
observed that she took a singular pleasure in talking upon it in all our succeeding
conferences when I thought proper to introduce it. The ball being ended, we went
to hear vespers at the church of the Canonesses, an order of nuns of which we
have none in France. These are young ladies who are entered in these communi-
ties at a tender age, in order to improve their fortunes till they are of an age to be
married. They do not all sleep under the same roof, but in detached houses within an enclosure. In each of these houses are three, four, or perhaps six young girls,
under the care of an old woman. These governesses, together with the abbess, are
of the number of such as have never been married. These girls never wear the
habit of the order but in church; and the service there ended, they dress like others, pay visits, frequent balls, and go where they please. They were constant visi-
tors at the Count's entertainments, and danced at his balls.

The Countess thought the time long until the night, when she had an opportunity of relating to the Count the conversation she had with me, and the opening
of the business. The next morning she came to me, and brought her husband with
her. He entered into a detail of the grievances the country laboured under, and
the just reasons he had for ridding it of the tyranny of Spain. In doing this, he
said, he should not consider himself as acting against his natural sovereign,
because he well knew he ought to look for him in the person of the King of
France. He explained to me the means whereby my brother might establish himself in Flanders, having possession of Hainault, which extended as far as Brussels.
He said the difficulty lay in securing the Cambresis, which is situated betwixt
Hainault and Flanders. It would, therefore, be necessary to engage M. d'Ainsi in
the business. To this I replied that, as he was his neighbour and friend, it might
be better that he should open the matter to him; and I begged he would do so. I
next assured him that he might have the most perfect reliance on the gratitude
and friendship of my brother, and be certain of receiving as large a share of power
and authority as such a service done by a person of his rank merited. Lastly, we
agreed upon an interview betwixt my brother and M. de Montigny, the brother

of the Count, which was to take place at La Fere, upon my return, when this business should be arranged. During the time I stayed at Mons, I said all I could to confirm the Count in this resolution, in which I found myself seconded by the Countess.

The day of my departure was now arrived, to the great regret of the ladies of Mons, as well as myself. The Countess expressed herself in terms which showed she had conceived the warmest friendship for me, and made me promise to return by way of that city. I presented the Countess with a diamond bracelet, and to the Count I gave a riband and diamond star of considerable value. But these presents, valuable as they were, became more so, in their estimation, as I was the donor.

Of the ladies, none accompanied me from this place, except Madame d'Aurec. She went with me to Namur, where I slept that night, and where she expected to find her husband and the Duc d'Arscot, her brother-in- law, who had been there since the peace betwixt the King of Spain and the States of Flanders. For though they were both of the party of the States, yet the Duc d'Arscot, being an old courtier and having attended King Philip in Flanders and England, could not withdraw himself from Court and the society of the great. The Comte de Lalain, with all his nobles, conducted me two leagues beyond his government, and until he saw Don John's company in the distance advancing to meet me. He then took his leave of me, being unwilling to meet Don John; but M. d'Ainsi stayed with me, as his master, the Bishop of Cambray, was in the Spanish interest.

This gallant company having left me, I was soon after met by Don John of Austria, preceded by a great number of running footmen, and escorted by only twenty or thirty horsemen. He was attended by a number of noblemen, and amongst the rest the Duc d'Arscot, M. d'Aurec, the Marquis de Varenbon, and the younger Balencon, governor, for the King of Spain, of the county of Burgundy. These last two, who are brothers, had ridden post to meet me. Of Don John's household there was only Louis de Gonzago of any rank. He called himself a relation of the Duke of Mantua; the others were mean-looking people, and of no consideration. Don John alighted from his horse to salute me in my litter, which was opened for the purpose. I returned the salute after the French fashion to him, the Duc d'Arscot, and M. d'Aurec. After an exchange of compliments, he mounted his horse, but continued in discourse with me until we reached the city, which was not before it grew dark, as I set off late, the ladies of Mons keeping me as long as they could, amusing themselves with viewing my litter, and requiring an explanation of the different mottoes and devices. However, as the Spaniards excel in preserving good order, Namur appeared with particular advantage, for the streets were well lighted, every house being illuminated, so that the blaze exceeded that of daylight.

Our supper was served to us in our respective apartments, Don John being unwilling, after the fatigue of so long a journey, to incommode us with a banquet. The house in which I was lodged had been newly furnished for the purpose of receiving me. It consisted of a magnificent large salon, with a private apartment, consisting of lodging rooms and closets, furnished in the most costly manner, with furniture of every kind, and hung with the richest tapestry of velvet and satin, divided into compartments by columns of silver embroidery, with knobs of gold, all wrought in the most superb manner. Within these compartments were figures in antique habits, embroidered in gold and silver.

The Cardinal de Lenoncourt, a man of taste and curiosity, being one day in these apartments with the Duc d'Arscot, who, as I have before observed, was an ornament to Don John's Court, remarked to him that this furniture seemed more proper for a great king than a young unmarried prince like Don John. To which the Duc d'Arscot replied that it came to him as a present, having been sent to him by a bashaw belonging to the Grand Seignior, whose son she had made prisoners in a signal victory obtained over the Turks. Don John having sent the bashaw's sons back without ransom, the father, in return, made him a present of a large quantity of gold, silver, and silk stuffs, which he caused to be wrought into tapestry at Milan, where there are curious workmen in this way; and he had the Queen's bedchamber hung with tapestry representing the battle in which he had so gloriously defeated the Turks.

The next morning Don John conducted us to chapel, where we heard mass celebrated after the Spanish manner, with all kinds of music, after which we partook of a banquet prepared by Don John. He and I were seated at a separate table, at a distance of three yards from which stood the great one, of which the honours were done by Madame d'Aurec. At this table the ladies and principal lords took their seats. Don John was served with drink by Louis de Gonzago, kneeling. The tables being removed, the ball was opened, and the dancing continued the whole afternoon. The evening was spent in conversation betwixt Don John and me, who told me I greatly resembled the Queen his mistress, by whom he meant the late Queen my sister, and for whom he professed to have entertained a very high esteem. In short, Don John manifested, by every mark of attention and politeness, as well to me as to my attendants, the very great pleasure he had in receiving me.

The boats which were to convey me upon the Meuse to Liege not all being ready, I was under the necessity of staying another day. The morning was passed as that of the day before. After dinner, we embarked on the river in a very beautiful boat, surrounded by others having on board musicians playing on hautboys, horns, and violins, and landed at an island where Don John had caused a collation to be prepared in a large bower formed with branches of ivy, in which the musicians were placed in small recesses, playing on their instruments during the time of supper. The tables being removed, the dances began, and lasted till it was time to return, which I did in the same boat that conveyed me thither, and which was that provided for my voyage.

The next morning Don John conducted me to the boat, and there took a most polite and courteous leave, charging M. and Madame d'Aurec to see me safe to Huy, the first town belonging to the Bishop of Liege, where I was to sleep. As soon as Don John had gone on shore, M. d'Ainsi, who remained in the boat, and who had the Bishop of Cambray's permission to go to Namur only, took leave of me with many protestations of fidelity and attachment to my brother and myself.

But Fortune, envious of my hitherto prosperous journey, gave me two omens of the sinister events of my return.

The first was the sudden illness which attacked Mademoiselle de Tournon, the daughter of the lady of my bedchamber, a young person, accomplished, with every grace and virtue, and for whom I had the most perfect regard. No sooner had the boat left the shore than this young lady was seized with an alarming disorder, which, from the great pain attending it, caused her to scream in the most doleful manner. The physicians attributed the cause to spasms of the heart, which, notwithstanding the utmost exertions of their skill, carried her off a few days after my arrival at Liege. As the history of this young lady is remarkable, I shall relate it in my next letter.

The other omen was what happened to us at Huy, immediately upon our arrival there. This town is built on the declivity of a mountain, at the foot of which runs the river Meuse. As we were about to land, there fell a torrent of rain, which, coming down the steep sides of the mountain, swelled the river instantly to such a degree that we had only time to leap out of the boat and run to the top, the flood reaching the very highest street, next to where I was to lodge. There we were forced to put up with such accommodation as could be procured in the house, as it was impossible to remove the smallest article of our baggage from the boats, or even to stir out of the house we were in, the whole city being under water. However, the town was as suddenly relieved from this calamity as it had been afflicted with it, for, on the next morning, the whole inundation had ceased, the waters having run off, and the river being confined within its usual channel.

Leaving Huy, M. and Madame d'Aurec returned to Don John at Namur, and I proceeded, in the boat, to sleep that night at Liege.

## LETTER XV.

*The City of Liege Described.—Affecting Story of Mademoiselle de Tournon.—Fatal Effects of Suppressed Anguish of Mind.*

The Bishop of Liege, who is the sovereign of the city and province, received me with all the cordiality and respect that could be expected from a personage of his dignity and great accomplishments. He was, indeed, a nobleman endowed with singular prudence and virtue, agreeable in his person and conversation, gracious and magnificent in his carriage and behaviour, to which I may add that he spoke the French language perfectly.

He was constantly attended by his chapter, with several of his canons, who are all sons of dukes, counts, or great German lords. The bishopric is itself a sovereign State, which brings in a considerable revenue, and includes a number of fine cities. The bishop is chosen from amongst the canons, who must be of noble descent, and resident one year. The city is larger than Lyons, and much resembles it, having the Meuse running through it. The houses in which the canons reside have the appearance of noble palaces.

The streets of the city are regular and spacious, the houses of the citizens well built, the squares large, and ornamented with curious fountains. The churches appear as if raised entirely of marble, of which there are considerable quarries in the neighbourhood; they are all of them ornamented with beautiful clocks, and exhibit a variety of moving figures.

The Bishop received me as I landed from the boat, and conducted me to his magnificent residence, ornamented with delicious fountains and gardens, set off with galleries, all painted, superbly gilt, and enriched with marble, beyond description.

The spring which affords the waters of Spa being distant no more than three or four leagues from the city of Liege, and there being only a village, consisting of three or four small houses, on the spot, the Princesse de Roche-sur-Yon was advised by her physicians to stay at Liege and have the waters brought to her, which they assured her would have equal efficacy, if taken after sunset and before sunrise, as if drunk at the spring. I was well pleased that she resolved to follow the advice of the doctors, as we were more comfortably lodged and had an agreeable society; for, besides his Grace (so the bishop is styled, as a king is addressed his Majesty, and a prince his Highness), the news of my arrival being spread about, many lords and ladies came from Germany to visit me. Amongst these was the Countess d'Aremberg, who had the honour to accompany Queen Elizabeth to Mezieres, to which place she came to marry King Charles my brother, a lady very high in the estimation of the Empress, the Emperor, and all the princes in Christendom. With her came her sister the Landgravine, Madame d'Aremberg her daughter, M. d'Aremberg her son, a gallant and accomplished nobleman, the perfect image of his father, who brought the Spanish succours to King Charles my brother, and returned with great honour and additional reputation. This meeting, so honourable to me, and so much to my satisfaction, was damped by the grief and concern occasioned by the loss of Mademoiselle de Tournon, whose story, being of a singular nature, I shall now relate to you, agreeably to the promise I made in my last letter.

I must begin with observing to you that Madame de Tournon, at this time lady of my bedchamber, had several daughters, the eldest of whom married M. de Balencon, governor, for the King of Spain, in the county of Burgundy. This daughter, upon her marriage, had solicited her mother to admit of her taking her sister, the young lady whose story I am now about to relate, to live with her, as she was going to a country strange to her, and wherein she had no relations. To this her mother consented; and the young lady, being universally admired for her modesty and graceful accomplishments, for which she certainly deserved admiration, attracted the notice of the Marquis de Varenbon. The Marquis, as I before mentioned, is the brother of M. de Balencon, and was intended for the Church; but, being violently enamoured of Mademoiselle de Tournon (whom, as he lived in the same house, he had frequent opportunities of seeing), he now begged his brother's permission to marry her, not having yet taken orders. The young lady's family, to whom he had likewise communicated his wish, readily gave their consent, but his brother refused his, strongly advising him to change his resolution and put on the gown.

Thus were matters situated when her mother, Madame de Tournon, a virtuous
and pious lady, thinking she had cause to be offended, ordered her daughter to
leave the house of her sister, Madame de Balencon, and come to her. The mother, a woman of a violent spirit, not considering that her daughter was grown up
and merited a mild treatment, was continually scolding the poor young lady, so
that she was for ever with tears in her eyes. Still, there was nothing to blame in
the young girl's conduct, but such was the severity of the mother's disposition.
The daughter, as you may well suppose, wished to be from under the mother's
tyrannical government, and was accordingly delighted with the thoughts of
attending me in this journey to Flanders, hoping, as it happened, that she should
meet the Marquis de Varenbon somewhere on the road, and that, as he had now
abandoned all thoughts of the Church, he would renew his proposal of marriage,
and take her from her mother.

I have before mentioned that the Marquis de Varenbon and the younger Balencon
joined us at Namur. Young Balencon, who was far from being so agreeable as his
brother, addressed himself to the young lady, but the Marquis, during the whole
time we stayed at Namur, paid not the least attention to her, and seemed as if he
had never been acquainted with her.

The resentment, grief, and disappointment occasioned by a behaviour so slight-
ing and unnatural was necessarily stifled in her breast, as decorum and her sex's
pride obliged her to appear as if she disregarded it; but when, after taking leave,
all of them left the boat, the anguish of her mind, which she had hitherto suppressed, could no longer be restrained, and, labouring for vent, it stopped her res-
piration, and forced from her those lamentable outcries which I have already spoken of. Her youth combated for eight days with this uncommon disorder, but at
the expiration of that time she died, to the great grief of her mother, as well as
myself. I say of her mother, for, though she was so rigidly severe over this daughter, she tenderly loved her.

The funeral of this unfortunate young lady was solemnised with all proper ceremonies, and conducted in the most honourable manner, as she was descended
from a great family, allied to the Queen my mother. When the day of interment
arrived, four of my gentlemen were appointed bearers, one of whom was named
La Boessiere. This man had entertained a secret passion for her, which he never
durst declare on account of the inferiority of his family and station. He was now
destined to bear the remains of her, dead, for whom he had long been dying, and
was now as near dying for her loss as he had before been for her love. The melancholy procession was marching slowly, along, when it was met by the Marquis de

Varenbon, who had been the sole occasion of it. We had not left Namur long when the Marquis reflected upon his cruel behaviour towards this unhappy young lady; and his passion (wonderful to relate) being revived by the absence of her who inspired it, though scarcely alive while she was present, he had resolved to come and ask her of her mother in marriage. He made no doubt, perhaps, of success, as he seldom failed in enterprises of love; witness the great lady he has since obtained for a wife, in opposition to the will of her family. He might, besides, have flattered himself that he should easily have gained a pardon from her by whom he was beloved, according to the Italian proverb, "Che la forza d'amore non riguarda al delitto" (Lovers are not criminal in the estimation of one another). Accordingly, the Marquis solicited Don John to be despatched to me on some errand, and arrived, as I said before, at the very instant the corpse of this ill-fated young lady was being borne to the grave. He was stopped by the crowd occasioned by this solemn procession. He contemplates it for some time. He observes a long train of persons in mourning, and remarks the coffin to be covered with a white pall, and that there are chaplets of flowers laid upon the coffin. He inquires whose funeral it is. The answer he receives is, that it is the funeral of a young lady. Unfortunately for him, this reply fails to satisfy his curiosity. He makes up to one who led the procession, and eagerly asks the name of the young lady they are proceeding to bury. When, oh, fatal answer! Love, willing to avenge the victim of his ingratitude and neglect, suggests a reply which had nearly deprived him of life. He no sooner hears the name of Mademoiselle de Tournon pronounced than he falls from his horse in a swoon. He is taken up for dead, and conveyed to the nearest house, where he lies for a time insensible; his soul, no doubt, leaving his body to obtain pardon from her whom he had hastened to a premature grave, to return to taste the bitterness of death a second time.

Having performed the last offices to the remains of this poor young lady, I was unwilling to discompose the gaiety of the society assembled here on my account by any show of grief. Accordingly, I joined the Bishop, or, as he is called, his Grace, and his canons, in their entertainments at different houses, and in gardens, of which the city and its neighbourhood afforded a variety. I was every morning attended by a numerous company to the garden, in which I drank the waters, the exercise of walking being recommended to be used with them. As the physician who advised me to take them was my own brother, they did not fail of their effect with me; and for these six or seven years which are gone over my head since I drank them, I have been free from any complaint of erysipelas on my arm. From this garden we usually proceeded to the place where we were invited to dinner. After dinner we were amused with a ball; from the ball we went to some convent, where we heard vespers; from vespers to supper, and that over, we had another ball, or music on the river.

# LETTER XVI.

*Queen Marguerite, on Her Return from Liege, Is in Danger of Being Made a Prisoner.—She Arrives, after Some Narrow Escapes, at La Fere.*

In this manner we passed the six weeks, which is the usual time for taking these waters, at the expiration of which the Princesse de Roche- sur-Yon was desirous to return to France; but Madame d'Aurec, who just then returned to us from Namur, on her way to rejoin her husband in Lorraine, brought us news of an extraordinary change of affairs in that town and province since we had passed through it.

It appeared from this lady's account that, on the very day we left Namur, Don John, after quitting the boat, mounted his horse under pretence of taking the diversion of hunting, and, as he passed the gate of the castle of Namur, expressed a desire of seeing it; that, having entered, he took possession of it, notwithstanding he held it for the States, agreeably to a convention. Don John, moreover, arrested the persons of the Duc d'Arscot and M. d'Aurec, and also made Madame d'Aurec a prisoner. After some remonstrances and entreaties, he had set her husband and brother-in- law at liberty, but detained her as a hostage for them. In consequence of these measures, the whole country was in arms. The province of Namur was divided into three parties: the first whereof was that of the States, or the Catholic party of Flanders; the second that of the Prince of Orange and the Huguenots; the third, the Spanish party, of which Don John was the head.

By letters which I received just at this time from my brother, through the hands of a gentleman named Lescar, I found I was in great danger of falling into the hands of one or other of these parties.

These letters informed me that, since my departure from Court, God had dealt favourably with my brother, and enabled him to acquit himself of the command of the army confided to him, greatly to the benefit of the King's service; so that he had taken all the towns and driven the Huguenots out of the provinces, agreeably to the design for which the army was raised; that he had returned to the Court at Poitiers, where the King stayed during the siege of Brouage, to be near to M. de Mayenne, in order to afford him whatever succours he stood in need of; that, as the Court is a Proteus, forever putting on a new face, he had found it entirely changed, so that he had been no more considered than if he had done the King no service whatever; and that Bussi, who had been so graciously looked upon before and during this last war, had done great personal service, and had lost a brother at the storming of Issoire, was very coolly received, and even as maliciously persecuted as in the time of Le Guast; in consequence of which either he or Bussi experienced some indignity or other. He further mentioned that the King's favourites had been practising with his most faithful servants, Maugiron, La Valette, Mauldon, and Hivarrot, and several other good and trusty men, to desert him, and enter into the King's service; and, lastly, that the King had repented of giving me leave to go to Flanders, and that, to counteract my brother, a plan was laid to intercept me on my return, either by the Spaniards, for which purpose they had been told that I had treated for delivering up the country to him, or by the Huguenots, in revenge of the war my brother had carried on against them, after having formerly assisted them.

This intelligence required to be well considered, as there seemed to be an utter impossibility of avoiding both parties. I had, however, the pleasure to think that two of the principal persons of my company stood well with either one or another party. The Cardinal de Lenoncourt had been thought to favour the Huguenot party, and M. Descarts, brother to the Bishop of Lisieux, was supposed to have the Spanish interest at heart. I communicated our difficult situation to the Princesse de Roche-sur-Yon and Madame de Tournon, who, considering that we could not reach La Fere in less than five or six days, answered me, with tears in their eyes, that God only had it in his power to preserve us, that I should recommend myself to his protection, and then follow such measures as should seem advisable. They observed that, as one of them was in a weak state of health, and the other advanced in years, I might affect to make short journeys on their account, and they would put up with every inconvenience to extricate me from the danger I was in.

I next consulted with the Bishop of Liege, who most certainly acted towards me like a father, and gave directions to the grand master of his household to attend me with his horses as far as I should think proper. As it was necessary that we should have a passport from the Prince of Orange, I sent Mondoucet to him to obtain one, as he was acquainted with the Prince and was known to favour his religion. Mondoucet did not return, and I believe I might have waited for him until this time to no purpose. I was advised by the Cardinal de Lenoncourt and my first esquire, the Chevalier Salviati, who were of the same party, not to stir without a passport; but, as I suspected a plan was laid to entrap me, I resolved to set out the next morning.

They now saw that this pretence was insufficient to detain me; accordingly, the Chevalier Salviati prevailed with my treasurer, who was secretly a Huguenot, to declare he had not money enough in his hands to discharge the expenses we had incurred at Liege, and that, in consequence, my horses were detained. I afterwards discovered that this was false, for, on my arrival at La Fere, I called for his accounts, and found he had then a balance in his hands which would have enabled him to pay, the expenses of my family for six or seven weeks. The Princesse de Roche-sur-Yon, incensed at the affront put upon me, and seeing the danger I incurred by staying, advanced the money that was required, to their great confusion; and I took my leave of his Grace the Bishop, presenting him with a diamond worth three thousand crowns, and giving his domestics gold chains and rings. Having thus taken our leave, we proceeded to Huy, without any other passport than God's good providence.

This town, as I observed before, belongs to the Bishop of Liege, but was now in a state of tumult and confusion, on account of the general revolt of the Low Countries, the townsmen taking part with the Netherlanders, notwithstanding the bishopric was a neutral State. On this account they paid no respect to the grand master of the Bishop's household, who accompanied us, but, knowing Don John had taken the castle of Namur in order, as they supposed, to intercept me on my return, these brutal people, as soon as I had got into my quarters, rang the alarm-bell, drew up their artillery, placed chains across the streets, and kept us thus confined and separated the whole night, giving us no opportunity to expostulate with them on such conduct. In the morning we were suffered to leave the town without further molestation, and the streets we passed through were lined with armed men.

From there we proceeded to Dinant, where we intended to sleep; but, unfortunately for us, the townspeople had on that day chosen their burghermasters, a kind of officers like the consuls in Gascony and France. In consequence of this election, it was a day of tumult, riot, and debauchery; every one in the town was drunk, no magistrate was acknowledged. In a word, all was in confusion. To render our situation still worse, the grand master of the Bishop's household had formerly done the town some ill office, and was considered as its enemy. The people of the town, when in their sober senses, were inclined to favour the party of the States, but under the influence of Bacchus they paid no regard to any party, not even to themselves.

As soon as I had reached the suburbs, they were alarmed at the number of my company, quitted the bottle and glass to take up their arms, and immediately shut the gates against me. I had sent a gentleman before me, with my harbinger and quartermasters, to beg the magistrates to admit me to stay one night in the town, but I found my officers had been put under an arrest. They bawled out to us from within, to tell us their situation, but could not make themselves heard. At length I raised myself up in my litter, and, taking off my mask, made a sign to a townsman nearest me, of the best appearance, that I was desirous to speak with him. As soon as he drew near me, I begged him to call out for silence, which being with some difficulty obtained, I represented to him who I was, and the occasion of my journey; that it was far from my intention to do them harm; but, to prevent any suspicions of the kind, I only begged to be admitted to go into their city with my women, and as few others of my attendants as they thought proper, and that we might be permitted to stay there for one night, whilst the rest of my company remained within the suburbs.

They agreed to this proposal, and opened their gates for my admission. I then entered the city with the principal persons of my company, and the grand master of the Bishop's household. This reverend personage, who was eighty years of age, and wore a beard as white as snow, which reached down to his girdle, this venerable old man, I say, was no sooner recognised by the drunken and armed rabble than he was accosted with the grossest abuse, and it was with difficulty they were restrained from laying violent hands upon him. At length I got him into my lodgings, but the mob fired at the house, the walls of which were only of plaster. Upon being thus attacked, I inquired for the master of the house, who, fortunately, was within. I entreated him to speak from the window, to some one without, to obtain permission for my being heard. I had some difficulty to get him to venture doing so. At length, after much bawling from the window, the burghermasters came to speak to me, but were so drunk that they scarcely knew what they said. I explained to them that I was entirely ignorant that the grand master of the Bishop's household was a person to whom they had a dislike, and I begged them to consider the consequences of giving offence to a person like me, who was a friend of the principal lords of the States, and I assured them that the Comte de Lalain, in particular, would be greatly displeased when he should hear how I had been received there.

The name of the Comte de Lalain produced an instant effect, much more than if I had mentioned all the sovereign princes I was related to. The principal person amongst them asked me, with some hesitation and stammering, if I was really a particular friend of the Count's. Perceiving that to claim kindred with the Count would do me more service than being related to all the Powers in Christendom, I answered that I was both a friend and a relation. They then made me many apologies and conges, stretching forth their hands in token of friendship; in short, they now behaved with as much civility as before with rudeness.

They begged my pardon for what had happened, and promised that the good old man, the grand master of the Bishop's household, should be no more insulted, but be suffered to leave the city quietly, the next morning, with me.

As soon as morning came, and while I was preparing to go to hear mass, there arrived the King's agent to Don John, named Du Bois, a man much attached to the Spanish interest. He informed me that he had received orders from the King my brother to conduct me in safety on my return. He said that he had prevailed on Don John to permit Barlemont to escort me to Namur with a troop of cavalry, and begged me to obtain leave of the citizens to admit Barlemont and his troop to enter the town that; they might receive my orders.

Thus had they concerted a double plot; the one to get possession of the town, the other of my person. I saw through the whole design, and consulted with the Cardinal de Lenoncourt, communicating to him my suspicions. The Cardinal was as unwilling to fall into the hands of the Spaniards as I could be; he therefore thought it advisable to acquaint the townspeople with the plot, and make our escape from the city by another road, in order to avoid meeting Barlemont's troop. It was agreed betwixt us that the Cardinal should keep Du Bois in discourse, whilst I consulted the principal citizens in another apartment.

Accordingly, I assembled as many as I could, to whom I represented that if they admitted Barlemont and his troop within the town, he would most certainly take possession of it for Don John. I gave it as my advice. to make a show of defence, to declare they would not be taken by surprise, and to offer to admit Barlemont, and no one else, within their gates. They resolved to act according to my counsel, and offered to serve me at the hazard of their lives. They promised to procure me a guide, who should conduct me by a road by following which I should put the river betwixt me and Don John's forces, whereby I should be out of his reach, and could be lodged in houses and towns which were in the interest of the States only.

This point being settled, I despatched them to give admission to M. de Barlemont, who, as soon as he entered within the gates, begged hard that his troop might come in likewise. Hereupon, the citizens flew into a violent rage, and were near putting him to death. They told him that if he did not order his men out of sight of the town, they would fire upon them with their great guns. This was done with design to give me time to leave the town before they could follow in pursuit of me. M. de Barlemont and the agent, Du Bois, used every argument they could devise to persuade me to go to Namur, where they said Don John waited to receive me.

I appeared to give way to their persuasions, and, after hearing mass and taking a hasty dinner, I left my lodgings, escorted by two or three hundred armed citizens, some of them engaging Barlemont and Du Bois in conversation. We all took the way to the gate which opens to the river, and directly opposite to that leading to Namur. Du Bois and his colleague told me I was not going the right way, but I continued talking, and as if I did not hear them. But when we reached the gate I hastened into the boat, and my people after me. M. de Barlemont and the agent Du Bois, calling out to me from the bank, told me I was doing very wrong and acting directly contrary to the King's intention, who had directed that I should return by way of Namur.

In spite of all their remonstrances we crossed the river with all possible expedition, and, during the two or three crossings which were necessary to convey over the litters and horses, the citizens, to give me the more time to escape, were debating with Barlemont and Du Bois concerning a number of grievances and complaints, telling them, in their coarse language, that Don John had broken the peace and falsified his engagements with the States; and they even rehearsed the old quarrel of the death of Egmont, and, lastly, declared that if the troop made its appearance before their walls again, they would fire upon it with their artillery.

I had by this means sufficient time to reach a secure distance, and was, by the help of God and the assistance of my guide, out of all apprehensions of danger from Barlemont and his troop.

I intended to lodge that night in a strong castle, called Fleurines, which belonged to a gentleman of the party of the States, whom I had seen with the Comte de Lalain. Unfortunately for me, the gentleman was absent, and his lady only was in the castle. The courtyard being open, we entered it, which put the lady into such a fright that she ordered the bridge to be drawn up, and fled to the strong tower.—[In the old French original, 'dongeon', whence we have 'duugeon'.]— Nothing we could say would induce her to give us entrance. In the meantime, three hundred gentlemen, whom Don John had sent off to intercept our passage, and take possession of the castle of Fleurines; judging that I should take up my quarters there, made their appearance upon an eminence, at the distance of about a thousand yards. They, seeing our carriages in the courtyard, and supposing that we ourselves had taken to the strong tower, resolved to stay where they were that night, hoping to intercept me the next morning.

In this cruel situation were we placed, in a courtyard surrounded by a wall by no means strong, and shut up by a gate equally as weak and as capable of being forced, remonstrating from time to time with the lady, who was deaf to all our prayers and entreaties.

Through God's mercy, her husband, M. de Fleurines, himself appeared just as night approached. We then gained instant admission, and the lady was greatly reprimanded by her husband for her incivility and indiscreet behaviour. This gentleman had been sent by the Comte de Lalain, with directions to conduct me through the several towns belonging to the States, the Count himself not being able to leave the army of the States, of which he had the chief command, to accompany me.

This was as favourable a circumstance for me as I could wish; for, M. de Fleurines offering to accompany me into France, the towns we had to pass through being of the party of the States, we were everywhere quietly and honourably received. I had only the mortification of not being able to visit Mons, agreeably to my promise made to the Comtesse de Lalain, not passing nearer to it than Nivelle, seven long leagues distant from it. The Count being at Antwerp, and the war being hottest in the neighbourhood of Mons, I thus was prevented seeing either of them on my return. I could only write to the Countess by a servant of the gentleman who was now my conductor. As soon as she learned I was at Nivelle, she sent some gentlemen, natives of the part of Flanders I was in, with a strong injunction to see me safe on the frontier of France.

I had to pass through the Cambresis, partly in favour of Spain and partly of the States. Accordingly, I set out with these gentlemen, to lodge at Cateau Cambresis. There they took leave of me, in order to return to Mons, and by them I sent the Countess a gown of mine, which had been greatly admired by her when I wore it at Mons; it was of black satin, curiously embroidered, and cost nine hundred crowns.

When I arrived at Cateau-Cambresis, I had intelligence sent me that a party of the Huguenot troops had a design to attack me on the frontiers of Flanders and

France. This intelligence I communicated to a few only of my company, and prepared to set off an hour before daybreak. When I sent for my litters and horses, I found much such a kind of delay from the Chevalier Salviati as I had before experienced at Liege, and suspecting it was done designedly, I left my litter behind, and mounted on horseback, with such of my attendants as were ready to follow me. By this means, with God's assistance, I escaped being waylaid by my enemies, and reached Catelet at ten in the morning. From there I went to my house at La Fere, where I intended to reside until I learned that peace was concluded upon.

At La Fere I found a messenger in waiting from my brother, who had orders to return with all expedition, as soon as I arrived, and inform him of it. My brother wrote me word, by that messenger, that peace was concluded, and the King returned to Paris; that, as to himself, his situation was rather worse than better; that he and his people were daily receiving some affront or other, and continual quarrels were excited betwixt the King's favourites and Bussi and my brother's principal attendants. This, he added, had made him impatient for my return, that he might come and visit me.

I sent his messenger back, and, immediately after, my brother sent Bussi and all his household to Angers, and, taking with him fifteen or twenty attendants, he rode post to me at La Fere. It was a great satisfaction to me to see one whom I so tenderly loved and greatly honoured, once more. I consider it amongst the greatest felicities I ever enjoyed, and, accordingly, it became my chief study to make his residence here agreeable to him. He himself seemed delighted with this change of situation, and would willingly have continued in it longer had not the noble generosity of his mind called him forth to great achievements. The quiet of our Court, when compared with that he had just left, affected him so powerfully that he could not but express the satisfaction he felt by frequently exclaiming, "Oh, Queen! how happy I am with you. My God! your society is a paradise wherein I enjoy every delight, and I seem to have lately escaped from hell, with all its furies and tortures!"

# LETTER XVII.

*Good Effects of Queen Marguerite's Negotiations in Flanders.— She Obtains Leave to Go to the King of Navarre Her Husband, but Her Journey Is Delayed.—Court Intrigues and Plots.—The Duc d'Alencon Again Put under Arrest.*

We passed nearly two months together, which appeared to us only as so many days. I gave him an account of what I had done for him in Flanders, and the state in which I had left the business. He approved of the interview with the Comte de Lalain's brother in order to settle the plan of operations and exchange assurances. Accordingly, the Comte de Montigny arrived, with four or five other leading men of the county of Hainault. One of these was charged with a letter from M. d'Ainsi, offering his services to my brother, and assuring him of the citadel of Cambray. M. de Montigny delivered his brother's declaration and engagement to give up the counties of Hainault and Artois, which included a number of fine cities. These offers made and accepted, my brother dismissed them with presents of gold medals, bearing his and my effigies, and every assurance of his future favour; and they returned to prepare everything for his coming. In the meanwhile my brother considered on the necessary measures to be used for raising a suffi-cient force, for which purpose he returned to the King, to prevail with him to assist him in this enterprise.

As I was anxious to go to Gascony, I made ready for the journey, and set off for Paris, my brother meeting me at the distance of one day's journey.

At St. Denis I was met by the King, the Queen my mother, Queen Louise, and the whole Court. It was at St. Denis that I was to stop and dine, and there it was that I had the honour of the meeting I have just mentioned.

I was received very graciously, and most sumptuously entertained. I was made to recount the particulars of my triumphant journey to Liege, and perilous return. The magnificent entertainments I had received excited their admiration, and they rejoiced at my narrow escapes. With such conversation I amused the Queen my mother and the rest of the company in her coach, on our way to Paris, where, supper and the ball being ended, I took an opportunity, when I saw the King and the Queen my mother together, to address them.

I expressed my hopes that they would not now oppose my going to the King my husband; that now, by the peace, the chief objection to it was removed, and if I delayed going, in the present situation of affairs, it might be prejudicial and discreditable to me. Both of them approved of my request, and commended my resolution. The Queen my mother added that she would accompany me on my journey, as it would be for the King's service that she did so. She said the King must furnish me with the necessary means for the journey, to which he readily assented. I thought this a proper time to settle everything, and prevent another journey to Court, which would be no longer pleasing after my brother left it, who was now pressing his expedition to Flanders with all haste. I therefore begged the Queen my mother to recollect the promise she had made my brother and me as soon as peace was agreed upon, which was that, before my departure for Gascony, I should have my marriage portion assigned to me in lands. She said that she recollected it well, and the King thought it very reasonable, and promised that it should be done. I entreated that it might be concluded speedily, as I wished to set off, with their permission, at the beginning of the next month. This, too, was granted me, but granted after the mode of the Court; that is to say, notwithstanding my constant solicitations, instead of despatch, I experienced only delay; and thus it continued for five or six months in negotiation.

My brother met with the like treatment, though he was continually urging the necessity for his setting out for Flanders, and representing that his expedition was for the glory and advantage of France,—for its glory, as such an enterprise would, like Piedmont, prove a school of war for the young nobility, wherein future Montlucs, Brissacs, Termes, and Bellegardes would be bred, all of them instructed in these wars, and afterwards, as field-marshals, of the greatest service to their country; and it would be for the advantage of France, as it would prevent civil wars; for Flanders would then be no longer a country wherein such discontented spirits as aimed at novelty could assemble to brood over their malice and hatch plots for the disturbance of their native land.

These representations, which were both reasonable and consonant with truth, had no weight when put into the scale against the envy excited by this advancement of my brother's fortune. Accordingly, every delay was used to hinder him from collecting his forces together, and stop his expedition to Flanders. Bussi and his other dependents were offered a thousand indignities. Every stratagem was tried, by day as well as by night, to pick quarrels with Bussi,—now by Quelus, at another time by Grammont, with the hope that my brother would engage in them. This was unknown to the King; but Maugiron, who had engrossed the King's favour, and who had quitted my brother's service, sought every means to ruin him, as it is usual for those who have given offence to hate the offended party.

Thus did this man take every occasion to brave and insult my brother; and relying upon the countenance and blind affection shown him by the King, had leagued himself with Quelus, Saint-Luc, Saint-Maigrin, Grammont, Mauleon, Hivarrot, and other young men who enjoyed the King's favour. As those who are favourites find a number of followers at Court, these licentious young courtiers thought they might do whatever they pleased. Some new dispute betwixt them and Bussi was constantly starting. Bussi had a degree of courage which knew not how to give way to any one; and my brother, unwilling to give umbrage to the King, and foreseeing that such proceedings would not forward his expedition, to avoid quarrels and, at the same time, to promote his plans, resolved to despatch Bussi to his duchy of Alencon, in order to discipline such troops as he should find there. My brother's amiable qualities excited the jealousy of Maugiron and the rest of his cabal about the King's person, and their dislike for Bussi was not so much on his own account as because he was strongly attached to my brother. The slights and disrespect shown to my brother were remarked by every one at Court; but his prudence, and the patience natural to his disposition, enabled him to put up with their insults, in hopes of finishing the business of his Flemish expedition, which would remove him to a distance from them and their machinations. This persecution was the more mortifying and discreditable as it even extended to his servants, whom they strove to injure by every means they could employ. M. de la Chastre at this time had a lawsuit of considerable consequence decided against him, because he had lately attached himself to my brother. At the instance of Maugiron and Saint-Luc, the King was induced to solicit the cause in favour of Madame de Senetaire, their friend. M. de la Chastre, being greatly injured by it, complained to my brother of the injustice done him, with all the concern such a proceeding may be supposed to have occasioned.

About this time Saint-Luc's marriage was celebrated. My brother resolved not to be present at it, and begged of me to join him in the same resolution. The Queen my mother was greatly uneasy on account of the behaviour of these young men, fearing that, if my brother did not join them in this festivity, it might be attended with some bad consequence, especially as the day was likely to produce scenes of revelry and debauch; she, therefore, prevailed on the King to permit her to dine on the wedding-day at St. Maur, and take my brother and me with her. This was the day before Shrove Tuesday; and we returned in the evening, the Queen my mother having well lectured my brother, and made him consent to appear at the ball, in order not to displease the King.

But this rather served to make matters worse than better, for Maugiron and his party began to attack him with such violent speeches as would have offended any one of far less consequence. They said he needed not to have given himself the trouble of dressing, for he was not missed in the afternoon; but now, they supposed, he came at night as the most suitable time; with other allusions to the meanness of his figure and smallness of stature. All this was addressed to the bride, who sat near him, but spoken out on purpose that he might hear it. My brother, perceiving this was purposely said to provoke an answer and occasion his giving offence to the King, removed from his seat full of resentment; and, consulting with M. de la Chastre, he came to the resolution of leaving the Court in a few days on a hunting party. He still thought his absence might stay their malice, and afford him an opportunity the more easily of settling his preparations for the Flemish expedition with the King. He went immediately to the Queen my mother, who was present at the ball, and was extremely sorry to learn what had happened, and imparted her resolution, in his absence, to solicit the King to hasten his expedition to Flanders. M. de Villequier being present, she bade him acquaint the King with my brother's intention of taking the diversion of hunting a few days; which she thought very proper herself, as it would put a stop to the disputes which had arisen betwixt him and the young men, Maugiron, Saint-Luc, Quelus, and the rest.

My brother retired to his apartment, and, considering his leave as granted, gave orders to his domestics to prepare to set off the next morning for St. Germain, where he should hunt the stag for a few days. He directed the grand huntsman to be ready with the hounds, and retired to rest, thinking to withdraw awhile from the intrigues of the Court, and amuse himself with the sports of the field. M. de Villequier, agreeably to the command he had received from the Queen my mother, asked for leave, and obtained it. The King, however, staying in his closet, like Rehoboam, with his council of five or six young men, they suggested suspicions in his mind respecting my brother's departure from Court. In short, they worked upon his fears and apprehensions so greatly, that he took one of the most rash and inconsiderate steps that was ever decided upon in our time; which was to put my brother and all his principal servants under an arrest. This measure was executed with as much indiscretion as it had been resolved upon. The King, under this agitation of mind, late as it was, hastened to the Queen my mother, and seemed as

if there was a general alarm and the enemy at the gates, for he exclaimed on seeing her: "How could you, Madame, think of asking me to let my brother go
hence? Do you not perceive how dangerous his going will prove to my kingdom?
Depend upon it that this hunting is merely a pretence to cover some treacherous
design. I am going to put him and his people under an arrest, and have his papers
examined. I am sure we shall make some great discoveries."

At the time he said this he had with him the Sieur de Cosse, captain of the guard,
and a number of Scottish archers. The Queen my mother, fearing, from the
King's haste and trepidation, that some mischief might happen to my brother,
begged to go with him. Accordingly, undressed as she was, wrapping herself up in
a night-gown, she followed the King to my brother's bedchamber. The King
knocked at the door with great violence, ordering it to be immediately opened,
for that he was there himself. My brother started up in his bed, awakened by the
noise, and, knowing that he had done nothing that he need fear, ordered Cange,
his valet de chambre, to open the door. The King entered in a great rage, and
asked him when he would have done plotting against him. "But I will show you,"
said he, "what it is to plot against your sovereign." Hereupon he ordered the
archers to take away all the trunks, and turn the valets de chambre out of the
room. He searched my brother's bed himself, to see if he could find any papers
concealed in it. My brother had that evening received a letter from Madame de
Sauves, which he kept in his hand, unwilling that it should be seen. The King
endeavoured to force it from him. He refused to part with it, and earnestly
entreated the King would not insist upon seeing it. This only excited the King's
anxiety the more to have it in his possession, as he now supposed it to be the key
to the whole plot, and the very document which would at once bring conviction
home to him. At length, the King having got it into his hands, he opened it in
the presence of the Queen my mother, and they were both as much confounded,
when they read the contents, as Cato was when he obtained a letter from Caesar,
in the Senate, which the latter was unwilling to give up; and which Cato, supposing it to contain a conspiracy against the Republic, found to be no other than
a love-letter from his own sister.

But the shame of this disappointment served only to increase the King's anger,
who, without condescending to make a reply to my brother, when repeatedly
asked what he had been accused of, gave him in charge of M. de Cosse and his
Scots, commanding them not to admit a single person to speak with him.

It was one o'clock in the morning when my brother was made a prisoner in the
manner I have now related. He feared some fatal event might succeed these violent proceedings, and he was under the greatest concern on my account, suppos-

ing me to be under a like arrest. He observed M. de Cosse to be much affected by the scene he had been witness to, even to shedding tears. As the archers were in the room he would not venture to enter into discourse with him, but only asked what was become of me. M. de Cosse answered that I remained at full liberty. My brother then said it was a great comfort to him to hear that news; "but," added he, "as I know she loves me so entirely that she would rather be confined with me than have her liberty whilst I was in confinement, I beg you will go to the Queen my mother, and desire her to obtain leave for my sister to be with me." He did so, and it was granted.

The reliance which my brother displayed upon this occasion in the sincerity of my friendship and regard for him conferred so great an obligation in my mind that, though I have received many particular favours since from him, this has always held the foremost place in my grateful remembrance.

By the time he had received permission for my being with him, daylight made its appearance. Seeing this, my brother begged M. de Cosse to send one of his archers to acquaint me with his situation, and beg me to come to him.

## LETTER XVIII.

*The Brothers Reconciled.—Alencon Restored to His Liberty.*

I was ignorant of what had happened to my brother, and when the Scottish archer came into my bedchamber, I was still asleep. He drew the curtains of the bed, and told me, in his broken French, that my brother wished to see me. I stared at the man, half awake as I was, and thought it a dream. After a short pause, and being thoroughly awakened, I asked him if he was not a Scottish archer. He answered me in the affirmative. "What!" cried I, "has my brother no one else to send a message by?" He replied he had not, for all his domestics had been put under an arrest. He then proceeded to relate, as well as he could explain himself, the events of the preceding night, and the leave granted my brother for my being with him during his imprisonment.

The poor fellow, observing me to be much affected by this intelligence, drew near, and whispered me to this purport: "Do not grieve yourself about this matter; I know a way of setting your brother at liberty, and you may depend upon it, that I will do it; but, in that case, I must go off with him." I assured him that he might rely upon being as amply rewarded as he could wish for such assistance, and, huddling on my clothes, I followed him alone to my brother's apartments. In going thither, I had occasion to traverse the whole gallery, which was filled with people, who, at another time, would have pressed forward to pay their respects to me; but, now that Fortune seemed to frown upon me, they all avoided me, or appeared as if they did not see me.

Coming into my brother's apartments, I found him not at all affected by what had happened; for such was the constancy of his mind, that his arrest had wrought no change, and he received me with his usual cheerfulness. He ran to meet me, and taking me in his arms, he said, "Queen! I beg you to dry up your tears; in my present situation, nothing can grieve me so much as to find you under any concern; for my own part, I am so conscious of my innocence and the integrity of my conduct, that I can defy the utmost malice of my enemies. If I should chance to fall the victim of their injustice, my death would prove a more cruel punishment to them than to me, who have courage sufficient to meet it in a just cause. It is not death I fear, because I have tasted sufficiently of the calamities and evils of life, and am ready to leave this world, which I have found only the abode of sorrow; but the circumstance I dread most is, that, not finding me sufficiently guilty to doom me to death, I shall be condemned to a long, solitary imprisonment; though I should even despise their tyranny in that respect, could I but have the assurance of being comforted by your presence."

These words, instead of stopping my tears, only served to make them stream afresh. I answered, sobbing, that my life and fortune were at his devotion; that the power of God alone could prevent me from affording him my assistance under every extremity; that, if he should be transported from that place, and I should be withheld from following him, I would kill myself on the spot.

Changing our discourse, we framed a number of conjectures on what might be the probable cause of the King's angry proceedings against him, but found ourselves at a loss what to assign them to.

Whilst we were discussing this matter the hour came for opening the palace gates, when a simple young man belonging to Bussi presented himself for entrance. Being stopped by the guard and questioned as to whither he was going, he, panic-struck, replied he was going to M. de Bussi, his master. This answer was carried to the King, and gave fresh grounds for suspicion. It seems my brother, supposing he should not be able to go to Flanders for some time, and resolving to send Bussi to his duchy of Alencon as I have already mentioned, had lodged him in the Louvre, that he might be near him to take instructions at every opportunity.

L'Archant, the general of the guard, had received the King's commands to make a search in the Louvre for him and Simier, and put them both under arrest. He entered upon this business with great unwillingness, as he was intimate with Bussi, who was accustomed to call him "father." L'Archant, going to Simier's apartment, arrested him; and though he judged Bussi was there too, yet, being unwilling to find him, he was going away. Bussi, however, who had concealed himself under the bed, as not knowing to whom the orders for his arrest might be given, finding he was to be left there, and sensible that he should be well treated by L'Archant, called out to him, as he was leaving the room, in his droll manner: "What, papa, are you going without me? Don't you think I am as great a rogue as that Simier?"

"Ah, son," replied L'Archant, "I would much rather have lost my arm than have met with you!"

Bussi, being a man devoid of all fear, observed that it was a sign that things went well with him; then, turning to Simier, who stood trembling with fear, he jeered him upon his pusillanimity. L'Archant removed them both, and set a guard over them; and, in the next place, proceeded to arrest M. de la Chastre, whom he took to the Bastille.

Meanwhile M. de l'Oste was appointed to the command of the guard which was set over my brother. This was a good sort of old man, who had been appointed governor to the King my husband, and loved me as if I had been his own child. Sensible of the injustice done to my brother and me, and lamenting the bad counsel by which the King was guided, and being, moreover, willing to serve us, he resolved to deliver my, brother from arrest. In order to make his intention known to us he ordered the Scottish archers to wait on the stairs without, keeping only, two whom he could trust in the room. Then taking me aside, he said:

"There is not a good Frenchman living who does not bleed at his heart to see what we see. I have served the King your father, and I am ready to lay down my life to serve his children. I expect to have the guard of the Prince your brother, wherever he shall chance to be confined; and, depend upon it, at the hazard of my life, I will restore him to his liberty. But," added he, "that no suspicions may arise that such is my design, it will be proper that we be not seen together in conversation; however, you may, rely upon my word."

This afforded me great consolation; and, assuming a degree of courage hereupon, I observed to my brother that we ought not to remain there without knowing for what reason we were detained, as if we were in the Inquisition; and that to treat us in such a manner was to consider us as persons of no account. I then begged M. de l'Oste to entreat the King, in our name, if the Queen our mother was not permitted to come to us, to send some one to acquaint us with the crime for which we were kept in confinement.

M. de Combaut, who was at the head of the young counsellors, was accordingly sent to us; and he, with a great deal of gravity, informed us that he came from the King to inquire what it was we wished to communicate to his Majesty. We answered that we wished to speak to some one near the King's person, in order to our being informed what we were kept in confinement for, as we were unable to assign any reason for it ourselves. He answered, with great solemnity, that we ought not to ask of God or the King reasons for what they did; as all their actions emanated from wisdom and justice. We replied that we were not persons to be treated like those shut up in the Inquisition, who are left to guess at the cause of their being there.

We could obtain from him, after all we said, no other satisfaction than his promise to interest himself in our behalf, and to do us all the service in his power. At this my brother broke out into a fit of laughter; but I confess I was too much alarmed to treat his message with such indifference, and could scarcely, refrain from talking to this messenger as he deserved.

Whilst he was making his report to the King, the Queen my mother kept her chamber, being under great concern, as may well be supposed, to witness such proceedings. She plainly foresaw, in her prudence, that these excesses would end fatally, should the mildness of my brother's disposition, and his regard for the welfare of the State, be once wearied out with submitting to such repeated acts of injustice. She therefore sent for the senior members of the Council, the chancellor, princes, nobles, and marshals of France, who all were greatly scandalised at the bad counsel which had been given to the King, and told the Queen my mother that she ought to remonstrate with the King upon the injustice of his proceedings. They observed that what had been done could not now be recalled, but matters might yet be set upon a right footing. The Queen my mother hereupon went to the King, followed by these counsellors, and represented to him the ill consequences which might proceed from the steps he had taken.

The King's eyes were by this time opened, and he saw that he had been ill advised. He therefore begged the Queen my mother to set things to rights, and to prevail on my brother to forget all that had happened, and to bear no resentment against these young men, but to make up the breach betwixt Bussi and Quelus.

Things being thus set to rights again, the guard which had been placed over my brother was dismissed, and the Queen my mother, coming to his apartment, told him he ought to return thanks to God for his deliverance, for that there had been a moment when even she herself despaired of saving his life; that since he must now have discovered that the King's temper of mind was such that he took the alarm at the very imagination of danger, and that, when once he was resolved upon a measure, no advice that she or any other could give would prevent him from putting it into execution, she would recommend it to him to submit himself to the King's pleasure in everything, in order to prevent the like in future; and, for the present, to take the earliest opportunity of seeing the King, and to appear as if he thought no more about the past.

We replied that we were both of us sensible of God's great mercy in delivering us from the injustice of our enemies, and that, next to God, our greatest obligation was to her; but that my brother's rank did not admit of his being put in confinement without cause, and released from it again without the formality of an acknowledgment. Upon this, the Queen observed that it was not in the power even of God himself to undo what had been done; that what could be effected to save his honour, and give him satisfaction for the irregularity of the arrest, should have place. My brother, therefore, she observed, ought to strive to mollify the King by addressing him with expressions of regard to his person and attachment to his service; and, in the meantime, use his influence over Bussi to reconcile him to Quelus, and to end all disputes betwixt them. She then declared that the principal motive for putting my brother and his servants under arrest was to prevent the combat for which old Bussi, the brave father of a brave son, had solicited the King's leave, wherein he proposed to be his son's second, whilst the father of Quelus was to be his. These four had agreed in this way to determine the matter in dispute, and give the Court no further disturbance.

My brother now engaged himself to the Queen that, as Bussi would see he could not be permitted to decide his quarrel by combat, he should, in order to deliver himself from his arrest, do as she had commanded.

The Queen my mother, going down to the King, prevailed with him to restore my brother to liberty with every honour. In order to which the King came to her apartment, followed by the princes, noblemen, and other members of the Council, and sent for us by M. de Villequier. As we went along we found all the rooms crowded with people, who, with tears in their eyes, blessed God for our deliverance. Coming into the apartments of the Queen my mother, we found the King attended as I before related. The King desired my brother not to take anything ill that had been done, as the motive for it was his concern for the good of his kingdom, and not any bad intention towards himself. My brother replied that he had, as he ought, devoted his life to his service, and, therefore, was governed by his pleasure; but that he most humbly begged him to consider that his fidelity and attachment did not merit the return he had met with; that, notwithstanding, he should impute it entirely to his own ill-fortune, and should be perfectly satisfied if the King acknowledged his innocence. Hereupon the King said that he entertained not the least doubt of his innocence, and only desired him to believe he held the same place in his esteem he ever had. The Queen my mother then, taking both of them by the hand, made them embrace each other.

Afterwards the King commanded Bussi to be brought forth, to make a reconciliation betwixt him and Quelus, giving orders, at the same time, for the release of Simier and M. de la Chastre. Bussi coming into the room with his usual grace, the King told him he must be reconciled with Quelus, and forbade him to say a word more concerning their quarrel. He then commanded them to embrace. "Sire," said Bussi, "if it is your pleasure that we kiss and are friends again, I am ready to obey your command;" then, putting himself in the attitude of Pantaloon, he went up to Queus and gave him a hug, which set all present in a titter, notwithstanding they had been seriously affected by the scene which had passed just before.

Many persons of discretion thought what had been done was too slight a reparation for the injuries my brother had received. When all was over, the King and the Queen my mother, coming up to me, said it would be incumbent on me to use my utmost endeavours to prevent my brother from calling to mind anything past which should make him swerve from the duty and affection he owed the King. I replied that my brother was so prudent, and so strongly attached to the King's service, that he needed no admonition on that head from me or any one else; and that, with respect to myself, I had never given him any other advice than to conform himself to the King's pleasure and the duty he owed him.

## LETTER XIX.

*The Duc d'Alencon Makes His Escape from Court.—Queen Marguerite's Fidelity Put to a Severe Trial.*

It was now three o'clock in the afternoon, and no one present had yet dined. The Queen my mother was desirous that we should eat together, and, after dinner, she ordered my brother and me to change our dress (as the clothes we had on were suitable only to our late melancholy situation) and come to the King's supper and ball. We complied with her orders as far as a change of dress, but our countenances still retained the impressions of grief and resentment which we inwardly felt.

I must inform you that when the tragi-comedy I have given you an account of was over, the Queen my mother turned round to the Chevalier de Seurre, whom she recommended to my brother to sleep in his bedchamber, and in whose conversation she sometimes took delight because he was a man of some humour, but rather inclined to be cynical.

"Well," said she, "M. de Seurre, what do you think of all this?"

"Madame, I think there is too much of it for earnest, and not enough for jest."

Then addressing himself to me, he said, but not loud enough for the Queen to hear him: "I do not believe all is over yet; I am very much mistaken if this young man" (meaning my brother) "rests satisfied with this." This day having passed in the manner before related, the wound being only skinned over and far from healed, the young men about the King's person set themselves to operate in order to break it out afresh.

These persons, judging of my brother by themselves, and not having sufficient experience to know the power of duty over the minds of personages of exalted rank and high birth, persuaded the King, still connecting his case with their own, that it was impossible my brother should ever forgive the affront he had received, and not seek to avenge himself with the first opportunity. The King, forgetting the ill-judged steps these young men had so lately induced him to take, hereupon receives this new impression, and gives orders to the officers of the guard to keep strict watch at the gates that his brother go not out, and that his people be made to leave the Louvre every evening, except such of them as usually slept in his bed-chamber or wardrobe.

My brother, seeing himself thus exposed to the caprices of these headstrong young fellows, who led the King according to their own fancies, and fearing something worse might happen than what he had yet experienced, at the end of three days, during which time he laboured under apprehensions of this kind, came to a determination to leave the Court, and never more return to it, but retire to his principality and make preparations with all haste for his expedition to Flanders. He communicated his design to me, and I approved of it, as I considered he had no other view in it than providing for his own safety, and that neither the King nor his government were likely to sustain any injury by it.

When we consulted upon the means of its accomplishment, we could find no other than his descending from my window, which was on the second story and opened to the ditch, for the gates were so closely watched that it was impossible to pass them, the face of every one going out of the Louvre being curiously examined. He begged of me, therefore, to procure for him a rope of sufficient strength and long enough for the purpose. This I set about immediately, for, having the sacking of a bed that wanted mending, I sent it out of the palace by a lad whom I could trust, with orders to bring it back repaired, and to wrap up the proper length of rope inside.

When all was prepared, one evening, at supper-time, I went to the Queen my mother, who supped alone in her own apartment, it being fast-day and the King eating no supper. My brother, who on most occasions was patient and discreet, spurred on by the indignities he had received, and anxious to extricate himself from danger and regain his liberty, came to me as I was rising from table, and whispered to me to make haste and come to him in my own apartment. M. de Matignon, at that time a marshal, a sly, cunning Norman, and one who had no love for my brother, whether he had some knowledge of his design from some one who could not keep a secret, or only guessed at it, observed to the Queen my

mother as she left the room (which I overheard, being near her, and circumspect-
ly watching every word and motion, as may well be imagined, situated as I was
betwixt fear and hope, and involved in perplexity) that my brother had undoubt-
edly an intention of withdrawing himself, and would not be there the next day;
adding that he was assured of it, and she might take her measures accordingly.

I observed that she was much disconcerted by this observation, and I had my fears
lest we should be discovered. When we came into her closet, she drew me aside
and asked if I heard what Matignon had said.

I replied: "I did not hear it, Madame, but I observe that it has given you uneasiness."

"Yes," said she, "a great deal of uneasiness, for you know I have pledged myself to
the King that your brother shall not depart hence, and Matignon has declared
that he knows very well he will not be here to-morrow."

I now found myself under a great embarrassment; I was in danger either of prov-
ing unfaithful to my brother, and thereby bringing his life into jeopardy, or of
being obliged to declare that to be truth which I knew to be false, and this I would
have died rather than be guilty of.

In this extremity, if I had not been aided by God, my countenance, without
speaking, would plainly have discovered what I wished to conceal. But God, who
assists those who mean well, and whose divine goodness was discoverable in my
brother's escape, enabled me to compose my looks and suggested to me such a
reply as gave her to understand no more than I wished her to know, and cleared
my conscience from making any declaration contrary to the truth. I answered her
in these words:

"You cannot, Madame, but be sensible that M. de Matignon is not one of my
brother's friends, and that he is, besides, a busy, meddling kind of man, who is
sorry to find a reconciliation has taken place with us; and, as to my brother, I will
answer for him with my life in case he goes hence, of which, if he had any design,
I should, as I am well assured, not be ignorant, he never having yet concealed anything he meant to do from me."

All this was said by me with the assurance that, after my brother's escape, they
would not dare to do me any injury; and in case of the worst, and when we should
be discovered, I had much rather pledge my life than hazard my soul by a false
declaration, and endanger my brother's life. Without scrutinising the import of

my speech, she replied: "Remember what you now say,—you will be bound for him on the penalty of your life."

I smiled and answered that such was my intention. Then, wishing her a good night, I retired to my own bedchamber, where, undressing myself in haste and getting into bed, in order to dismiss the ladies and maids of honour, and there then remaining only my chamber-women, my brother came in, accompanied by Simier and Cange. Rising from my bed, we made the cord fast, and having looked out, at the window to discover if any one was in the ditch, with the assistance of three of my women, who slept in my room, and the lad who had brought in the rope, we let down my brother, who laughed and joked upon the occasion without the least apprehension, notwithstanding the height was considerable. We next lowered Simier into the ditch, who was in such a fright that he had scarcely strength to hold the rope fast; and lastly descended my brother's valet de chambre, Cange.

Through God's providence my brother got off undiscovered, and going to Ste. Genevieve, he found Bussi waiting there for him. By consent of the abbot, a hole had been made in the city wall, through which they passed, and horses being provided and in waiting, they mounted, and reached Angers without the least accident.

Whilst we were lowering down Cange, who, as I mentioned before, was the last, we observed a man rising out of the ditch, who ran towards the lodge adjoining to the tennis-court, in the direct way leading to the guard-house. I had no apprehensions on my own account, all my fears being absorbed by those I entertained for my brother; and now I was almost dead with alarm, supposing this might be a spy placed there by M. de Matignon, and that my brother would be taken. Whilst I was in this cruel state of anxiety, which can be judged of only by those who have experienced a similar situation, my women took a precaution for my safety and their own, which did not suggest itself to me. This was to burn the rope, that it might not appear to our conviction in case the man in question had been placed there to watch us. This rope occasioned so great a flame in burning, that it set fire to the chimney, which, being seen from without, alarmed the guard, who ran to us, knocking violently at the door, calling for it to be opened.

I now concluded that my brother was stopped, and that we were both undone. However, as, by the blessing of God and through his divine mercy alone, I have, amidst every danger with which I have been repeatedly surrounded, constantly preserved a presence of mind which directed what was best to be done, and observing that the rope was not more than half consumed, I told my women to go to the door, and speaking softly, as if I was asleep, to ask the men what they wanted. They did so, and the archers replied that the chimney was on fire, and they came to extinguish it. My women answered it was of no consequence, and they could put it out themselves, begging them not to awake me. This alarm thus passed off quietly, and they went away; but, in two hours afterward, M. de Cosse came for me to go to the King and the Queen, my mother, to give an account of my brother's escape, of which they had received intelligence by the Abbot of Ste. Genevieve.

It seems it had been concerted betwixt my brother and the abbot, in order to prevent the latter from falling under disgrace, that, when my brother might be supposed to have reached a sufficient distance, the abbot should go to Court, and say that he had been put into confinement whilst the hole was being made, and that he came to inform the King as soon as he had released himself.

I was in bed, for it was yet night; and rising hastily, I put on my night-clothes. One of my women was indiscreet enough to hold me round the waist, and exclaim aloud, shedding a flood of tears, that she should never see me more. M. de Cosse, pushing her away, said to me: "If I were not a person thoroughly devoted to your service, this woman has said enough to bring you into trouble. But," continued he, "fear nothing. God be praised, by this time the Prince your brother is out of danger."

These words were very necessary, in the present state of my mind, to fortify it against the reproaches and threats I had reason to expect from the King. I found him sitting at the foot of the Queen my mother's bed, in such a violent rage that I am inclined to believe I should have felt the effects of it, had he not been restrained by the absence of my brother and my mother's presence. They both told me that I had assured them my brother would not leave the Court, and that I pledged myself for his stay. I replied that it was true that he had deceived me, as he had them; however, I was ready still to pledge my life that his departure would not operate to the prejudice of the King's service, and that it would appear he was only gone to his own principality to give orders and forward his expedition to Flanders.

The King appeared to be somewhat mollified by this declaration, and now gave me permission to return to my own apartments. Soon afterwards he received letters from my brother, containing assurances of his attachment, in the terms I had before expressed. This caused a cessation of complaints, but by no means removed the King's dissatisfaction, who made a show of affording assistance to his expedition, but was secretly using every means to frustrate and defeat it.

# LETTER XX.

*Queen Marguerite Permitted to Go to the King Her Husband.—Is Accompanied by the Queenmother.—Marguerite Insulted by Her Husband's Secretary.— She Harbours Jealousy.—Her Attention to the King Her Husband during an Indisposition.—Their Reconciliation.—The War Breaks Out Afresh.— Affront Received from Marechal de Biron.*

I now renewed my application for leave to go to the King my husband, which I continued to press on every opportunity. The King, perceiving that he could not refuse my leave any longer, was willing I should depart satisfied. He had this further view in complying with my wishes, that by this means he should withdraw me from my attachment to my brother. He therefore strove to oblige me in every way he could think of, and, to fulfil the promise made by the Queen my mother at the Peace of Sens, he gave me an assignment of my portion in territory, with the power of nomination to all vacant benefices and all offices; and, over and above the customary pension to the daughters of France, he gave another out of his privy purse.

He daily paid me a visit in my apartment, in which he took occasion to represent to me how useful his friendship would be to me; whereas that of my brother could be only injurious,—with arguments of the like kind.

However, all he could say was insufficient to prevail on me to swerve from the fidelity I had vowed to observe to my brother. The King was able to draw from me no other declaration than this: that it ever was, and should be, my earnest wish to see my brother firmly established in his gracious favour, which he had never appeared to me to have forfeited; that I was well assured he would exert himself to the utmost to regain it by every act of duty and meritorious service; that, with respect to myself, I thought I was so much obliged to him for the great honour he did me by repeated acts of generosity, that he might be assured, when I was with the King my husband I should consider myself bound in duty to obey all such commands as he should be pleased to give me; and that it would be my whole study to maintain the King my husband in a submission to his pleasure.

My brother was now on the point of leaving Alencon to go to Flanders; the Queen my mother was desirous to see him before his departure. I begged the King to permit me to take the opportunity of accompanying her to take leave of my brother, which he granted; but, as it seemed, with great unwillingness. When we returned from Alencon, I solicited the King to permit me to take leave of himself, as I had everything prepared for my journey. The Queen my mother being desirous to go to Gascony, where her presence was necessary for the King's service, was unwilling that I should depart without her. When we left Paris, the King accompanied us on the way as far as his palace of Dolinville. There we stayed with him a few days, and there we took our leave, and in a little time reached Guienne, which belonging to, and being under the government of the King my husband, I was everywhere received as Queen. My husband gave the Queen my mother a meeting at Wolle, which was held by the Huguenots as a cautionary town; and the country not being sufficiently quieted, she was permitted to go no further.

It was the intention of the Queen my mother to make but a short stay; but so many accidents arose from disputes betwixt the Huguenots and Catholics, that she was under the necessity of stopping there eighteen months. As this was very much against her inclination, she was sometimes inclined to think there was a design to keep her, in order to have the company of her maids of honour. For my husband had been greatly smitten with Dayelle, and M. de Thurene was in love with La Vergne. However, I received every mark of honour and attention from the King that I could expect or desire. He related to me, as soon as we met, the artifices which had been put in practice whilst he remained at Court to create a misunderstanding betwixt him and me; all this, he said, he knew was with a design to cause a rupture betwixt my brother and him, and thereby ruin us all three, as there was an exceeding great jealousy entertained of the friendship which existed betwixt us.

We remained in the disagreeable situation I have before described all the time the Queen my mother stayed in Gascony; but, as soon as she could reestablish peace, she, by desire of the King my husband, removed the King's lieutenant, the Marquis de Villars, putting in his place the Marechal de Biron. She then departed for Languedoc, and we conducted her to Castelnaudary; where, taking our leave, we returned to Pau, in Bearn; in which place, the Catholic religion not being tolerated, I was only allowed to have mass celebrated in a chapel of about three or four feet in length, and so narrow that it could scarcely hold seven or eight persons. During the celebration of mass, the bridge of the castle was drawn up to prevent the Catholics of the town and country from coming to assist at it; who having been, for some years, deprived of the benefit of following their own mode of worship, would have gladly been present. Actuated by so holy and laudable a desire, some of the inhabitants of Pau, on Whitsunday, found means to get into the castle before the bridge was drawn up, and were present at the celebration of mass, not being discovered until it was nearly over. At length the Huguenots espied them, and ran to acquaint Le Pin, secretary to the King my, husband, who was greatly in his favour, and who conducted the whole business relating to the new religion. Upon receiving this intelligence, Le Pin ordered the guard to arrest these poor people, who were severely beaten in my presence, and afterwards locked up in prison, whence they were not released without paying a considerable fine.

This indignity gave me great offence, as I never expected anything of the kind. Accordingly, I complained of it to the King my husband, begging him to give orders for the release of these poor Catholics, who did not deserve to be punished for coming to my chapel to hear mass, a celebration of which they had been so long deprived of the benefit. Le Pin, with the greatest disrespect to his master, took upon him to reply, without waiting to hear what the King had to say. He told me that I ought not to trouble the King my husband about such matters; that what had been done was very right and proper; that those people had justly merited the treatment they met with, and all I could say would go for nothing, for it must be so; and that I ought to rest satisfied with being permitted to have mass said to me and my servants. This insolent speech from a person of his inferior condition incensed me greatly, and I entreated the King my husband, if I had the least share in his good graces, to do me justice, and avenge the insult offered me by this low man.

The King my husband, perceiving that I was offended, as I had reason to be, with this gross indignity, ordered Le Pin to quit our presence immediately; and, expressing his concern at his secretary's behaviour, who, he said, was overzealous in the cause of religion, he promised that he would make an example of him. As to the Catholic prisoners, he said he would advise with his parliament what ought to be done for my satisfaction.

Having said this, he went to his closet, where he found Le Pin, who, by dint of persuasion, made him change his resolution; insomuch that, fearing I should insist upon his dismissing his secretary, he avoided meeting me. At last, finding that I was firmly resolved to leave him, unless he dismissed Le Pin, he took advice of some persons, who, having themselves a dislike to the secretary, represented that he ought not to give me cause of displeasure for the sake of a man of his small importance,—especially one who, like him, had given me just reason to be offended; that, when it became known to the King my brother and the Queen my mother, they would certainly take it ill that he had not only not resented it, but, on the contrary, still kept him near his person.

This counsel prevailed with him, and he at length discarded his secretary. The King, however, continued to behave to me with great coolness, being influenced, as he afterwards confessed, by the counsel of M. de Pibrac, who acted the part of a double dealer, telling me that I ought not to pardon an affront offered by such a mean fellow, but insist upon his being dismissed; whilst he persuaded the King my husband that there was no reason for parting with a man so useful to him, for such a trivial cause. This was done by M. de Pibrac, thinking I might be induced, from such mortifications, to return to France, where he enjoyed the offices of president and King's counsellor.

I now met with a fresh cause for disquietude in my present situation, for, Dayelle being gone, the King my husband placed his affections on Rebours. She was an artful young person, and had no regard for me; accordingly, she did me all the ill offices in her power with him. In the midst of these trials, I put my trust in God, and he, moved with pity by my tears, gave permission for our leaving Pau, that "little Geneva;" and, fortunately for me, Rebours was taken ill and stayed behind. The King my husband no sooner lost sight of her than he forgot her; he now turned his eyes and attention towards Fosseuse. She was much handsomer than the other, and was at that time young, and really a very amiable person.

Pursuing the road to Montauban, we stopped at a little town called Eause, where, in the night, the King my husband was attacked with a high fever, accompanied with most violent pains in his head. This fever lasted for seventeen days, during which time he had no rest night or day, but was continually removed from one bed to another. I nursed him the whole time, never stirring from his bedside, and never putting off my clothes. He took notice of my extraordinary tenderness, and spoke of it to several persons, and particularly to my cousin M———, who, acting the part of an affectionate relation, restored me to his favour, insomuch that I never stood so highly in it before. This happiness I had the good fortune to enjoy during the four or five years that I remained with him in Gascony.

Our residence, for the most part of the time I have mentioned, was at Nerac, where our Court was so brilliant that we had no cause to regret our absence from the Court of France. We had with us the Princesse de Navarre, my husband's sister, since married to the Duc de Bar; there were besides a number of ladies belonging to myself. The King my husband was attended by a numerous body of lords and gentlemen, all as gallant persons as I have seen in any Court; and we had only to lament that they were Huguenots. This difference of religion, however, caused no dispute among us; the King my husband and the Princess his sister heard a sermon, whilst I and my servants heard mass. I had a chapel in the park for the purpose, and, as soon as the service of both religions was over, we joined company in a beautiful garden, ornamented with long walks shaded with laurel and cypress trees. Sometimes we took a walk in the park on the banks of the river, bordered by an avenue of trees three thousand yards in length. The rest of the day was passed in innocent amusements; and in the afternoon, or at night, we commonly had a ball.

The King was very assiduous with Fosseuse, who, being dependent on me, kept herself within the strict bounds of honour and virtue. Had she always done so, she had not brought upon herself a misfortune which has proved of such fatal consequence to myself as well as to her.

But our happiness was too great to be of long continuance, and fresh troubles broke out betwixt the King my husband and the Catholics, and gave rise to a new war. The King my husband and the Marechal de Biron, who was the King's lieutenant in Guienne, had a difference, which was aggravated by the Huguenots. This breach became in a short time so wide that all my efforts to close it were useless. They made their separate complaints to the King. The King my husband insisted on the removal of the Marechal de Biron, and the Marshal charged the King my husband, and the rest of those who were of the pretended reformed religion, with designs contrary to peace. I saw, with great concern, that affairs were likely soon to come to an open rupture; and I had no power to prevent it.

The Marshal advised the King to come to Guienne himself, saying that in his presence matters might be settled. The Huguenots, hearing of this proposal, supposed the King would take possession of their towns, and, thereupon, came to a resolution to take up arms. This was what I feared; I was become a sharer in the King my husband's fortune, and was now to be in opposition to the King my brother and the religion I had been bred up in. I gave my opinion upon this war to the King my husband and his Council, and strove to dissuade them from engaging in it. I represented to them the hazards of carrying on a war when they were to be opposed against so able a general as the Marechal de Biron, who would not spare them, as other generals had done, he being their private enemy. I begged them to consider that, if the King brought his whole force against them, with intention to exterminate their religion, it would not be in their power to oppose or prevent it. But they were so headstrong, and so blinded with the hope of succeeding in the surprise of certain towns in Languedoc and Gascony, that, though the King did me the honour, upon all occasions, to listen to my advice, as did most of the Huguenots, yet I could not prevail on them to follow it in the present situation of affairs, until it was too late, and after they had found, to their cost, that my counsel was good. The torrent was now burst forth, and there was no possibility of stopping its course until it had spent its utmost strength.

Before that period arrived, foreseeing the consequences, I had often written to the King and the Queen my mother, to offer something to the King my husband by way of accommodating matters. But they were bent against it, and seemed to be pleased that matters had taken such a turn, being assured by Marechal de Biron that he had it in his power to crush the Huguenots whenever he pleased. In this crisis my advice was not attended to, the dissensions increased, and recourse was had to arms.

The Huguenots had reckoned upon a force more considerable than they were able to collect together, and the King my husband found himself outnumbered by Marechal de Biron. In consequence, those of the pretended reformed religion failed in all their plans, except their attack upon Cahors, which they took with petards, after having lost a great number of men, M. de Vezins, who commanded in the town, disputing their entrance for two or three days, from street to street, and even from house to house. The King my husband displayed great valour and conduct upon the. occasion, and showed himself to be a gallant and brave general. Though the Huguenots succeeded in this attempt, their loss was so great that they gained nothing from it. Marechal de Biron kept the field, and took every place that declared for the Huguenots, putting all that opposed him to the sword.

From the commencement of this war, the King my husband doing me the honour to love me, and commanding me not to leave him, I had resolved to share his fortune, not without extreme regret, in observing that this war was of such a nature that I could not, in conscience, wish success to either side; for if the Huguenots got the upper hand, the religion which I cherished as much as my life was lost, and if the Catholics prevailed, the King my husband was undone. But, being thus attached to my husband, by the duty I owed him, and obliged by the attentions he was pleased to show me, I could only acquaint the King and the Queen my mother with the situation to which I was reduced, occasioned by my advice to them not having been attended to. I, therefore, prayed them, if they could not extinguish the flames of war in the midst of which I was placed, at least to give orders to Marechal de Biron to consider the town I resided in, and three leagues round it, as neutral ground, and that I would get the King my husband to do the same. This the King granted me for Nerac, provided my husband was not there; but if he should enter it, the neutrality was to cease, and so to remain as long as he continued there. This convention was observed, on both sides, with all the exactness I could desire. However, the King my husband was not to be prevented from often visiting Nerac, which was the residence of his sister and me. He was fond of the society of ladies, and, moreover, was at that time greatly enamoured with Fosseuse, who held the place in his affections which Rebours had lately occupied. Fosseuse did me no ill offices, so that the King my husband and I continued to live on very good terms, especially as he perceived me unwilling to oppose his inclinations.

Led by such inducements, he came to Nerac, once, with a body of troops, and stayed three days, not being able to leave the agreeable company he found there. Marechal de Biron, who wished for nothing so much as such an opportunity, was apprised of it, and, under pretence of joining M. de Cornusson, the seneschal of Toulouse, who was expected with a reinforcement for his army, he began his march; but, instead of pursuing the road, according to the orders he had issued, he suddenly ordered his troops to file off towards Nerac, and, before nine in the morning, his whole force was drawn up within sight of the town, and within cannon-shot of it.

The King my husband had received intelligence, the evening before, of the expected arrival of M. de Cornusson, and was desirous of preventing the junction, for which purpose he resolved to attack him and the Marshal separately. As he had been lately joined by M. de La Rochefoucauld, with a corps of cavalry consisting of eight hundred men, formed from the nobility of Saintonge, he found himself sufficiently strong to undertake such a plan. He, therefore, set out before break of day to make his attack as they crossed the river. But his intelligence did not prove to be correct, for De Cornusson passed it the evening before. My husband, being thus disappointed in his design, returned to Nerac, and entered at one gate just as Marechal de Biron drew up his troops before the other. There fell so heavy a rain at that moment that the musketry was of no use. The King my husband, however, threw a body of his troops into a vineyard to stop the Marshal's progress, not being able to do more on account of the unfavourableness of the weather.

In the meantime, the Marshal continued with his troops drawn up in order of battle, permitting only two or three of his men to advance, who challenged a like number to break lances in honour of their mistresses. The rest of the army kept their ground, to mask their artillery, which, being ready to play, they opened to the right and left, and fired seven or eight shots upon the town, one of which struck the palace. The Marshal, having done this, marched off, despatching a trumpeter to me with his excuse. He acquainted me that, had I been alone, he would on no account have fired on the town; but the terms of neutrality for the town, agreed upon by the King, were, as I well knew, in case the King my husband should not be found in it, and, if otherwise, they were void. Besides which, his orders were to attack the King my husband wherever he should find him.

I must acknowledge on every other occasion the Marshal showed me the greatest respect, and appeared to be much my friend. During the war my letters have frequently fallen into his hands, when he as constantly forwarded them to me unopened. And whenever my people have happened to be taken prisoners by his army, they were always well treated as soon as they mentioned to whom they belonged.

I answered his message by the trumpeter, saying that I well knew what he had done was strictly agreeable to the convention made and the orders he had received, but that a gallant officer like him would know how to do his duty without giving his friends cause of offence; that he might have permitted me the enjoyment of the King my husband's company in Nerac for three days, adding, that he could not attack him, in my presence, without attacking me; and concluding that, certainly, I was greatly offended by his conduct, and would take the first opportunity of making my complaint to the King my brother.

# LETTER XXI.

*Situation of Affairs in Flanders.—Peace Brought About by Duc d'Alencon's Negotiation.—Marechal de Biron Apologises for Firing on Nerac.—Henri Desperately in Love with Fosseuse.—Queen Marguerite Discovers Fosseuse to Be Pregnant, Which She Denies.—Fosseuse in Labour. Marguerite's Generous Behaviour to Her.— Marguerite's Return to Paris.*

The war lasted some time longer, but with disadvantage to the Huguenots. The King my husband at length became desirous to make a peace. I wrote on the subject to the King and the Queen my mother; but so elated were they both with Marechal de Biron's success that they would not agree to any terms.

About the time this war broke out, Cambray, which had been delivered up to my brother by M. d'Ainsi, according to his engagement with me, as I have before related, was besieged by the forces of Spain. My brother received the news of this siege at his castle of Plessis-les-Tours, whither he had retired after his return from Flanders, where, by the assistance of the Comte de Lalain, he had been invested with the government of Mons, Valenciennes, and their dependencies.

My brother, being anxious to relieve Cambray, set about raising an army, with all the expedition possible; but, finding it could not be accomplished very speedily, he sent forward a reinforcement under the command of M. de Balagny, to succour the place until he arrived himself with a sufficient force to raise the siege. Whilst he was in the midst of these preparations this Huguenot war broke out, and the men he had raised left him to incorporate themselves with the King's army, which had reached Gascony.

My brother was now without hope of raising the siege, and to lose Cambray would be attended with the loss of the other countries he had just obtained. Besides, what he should regret more, such losses would reduce to great straits M. de Balagny and the gallant troops so nobly defending the place.

His grief on this occasion was poignant, and, as his excellent judgment furnished him with expedients under all his difficulties, he resolved to endeavour to bring about a peace. Accordingly he despatched a gentleman to the King with his advice to accede to terms, offering to undertake the treaty himself. His design in offering himself as negotiator was to prevent the treaty being drawn out to too great a length, as might be the case if confided to others. It was necessary that he should speedily relieve Cambray, for M. de Balagny, who had thrown himself into the city as I have before mentioned, had written to him that he should be able to defend the place for six months; but, if he received no succours within that time, his provisions would be all expended, and he should be obliged to give way to the clamours of the inhabitants, and surrender the town.

By God's favour, the King was induced to listen to my brother's proposal of undertaking a negotiation for a peace. The King hoped thereby to disappoint him in his expectations in Flanders, which he never had approved. Accordingly he sent word back to my brother that he should accept his proffer of negotiating a peace, and would send him for his coadjutors, M. de Villeroy and M. de Bellievre. The commission my brother was charged with succeeded, and, after a stay of seven months in Gascony, he settled a peace and left us, his thoughts being employed during the whole time on the means of relieving Cambray, which the satisfaction he found in being with us could not altogether abate.

The peace my brother, made, as I have just mentioned, was so judiciously framed that it gave equal satisfaction to the King and the Catholics, and to the King my husband and the Huguenots, and obtained him the affections of both parties. He likewise acquired from it the assistance of that able general, Marechal de Biron, who undertook the command of the army destined to raise the siege of Cambray. The King my husband was equally gratified in the Marshal's removal from Gascony and having Marechal de Matignon in his place.

Before my brother set off he was desirous to bring about a reconciliation betwixt the King my husband and Mareohal de Biron, provided the latter should make his apologies to me for his conduct at Nerac. My brother had desired me to treat him with all disdain, but I used this hasty advice with discretion, considering that my brother might one day or other repent having given it, as he had everything to hope, in his present situation, from the bravery of this officer.

My brother returned to France accompanied by Marechal de Biron. By his nego-tiation of a peace he had acquired to himself great credit with both parties, and secured a powerful force for the purpose of raising the siege of Cambray. But hon-ours and success are followed by envy. The King beheld this accession of glory to his brother with great dissatisfaction. He had been for seven months, while my brother and I were together in Gascony, brooding over his malice, and produced the strangest invention that can be imagined. He pretended to believe (what the King my husband can easily prove to be false) that I instigated him to go to war that I might procure for my brother the credit of making peace. This is not at all probable when it is considered the prejudice my brother's affairs in, Flanders sus-tained by the war.

But envy and malice are self-deceivers, and pretend to discover what no one else can perceive. On this frail foundation the King raised an altar of hatred, on which he swore never to cease till he had accomplished my brother's ruin and mine. He had never forgiven me for the attachment I had discovered for my brother's inter-est during the time he was in Poland and since.

Fortune chose to favour the King's animosity; for, during the seven months that my brother stayed in Gascony, he conceived a passion for Fosseuse, who was become the doting piece of the King my husband, as I have already mentioned, since he had quitted Rebours. This new passion in my brother had induced the King my husband to treat me with coldness, supposing that I countenanced my brother's addresses. I no sooner discovered this than I remonstrated with my brother, as I knew he would make every sacrifice for my repose. I begged him to give over his pursuit, and not to speak to her again. I succeeded this way to defeat the malice of my ill-fortune; but there was still behind another secret ambush, and that of a more fatal nature; for Fosseuse, who was passionately fond of the King my husband, but had hitherto granted no favours inconsistent with prudence and modesty, piqued by his jealousy of my brother, gave herself up suddenly to his will, and unfortunately became pregnant. She no sooner made this discovery, than she altered her conduct towards me entirely from what it was before. She now shunned my presence as much as she had been accustomed to seek it, and where-as before she strove to do me every good office with the King my husband, she now endeavoured to make all the mischief she was able betwixt us. For his part, he avoided me; he grew cold and indifferent, and since Fosseuse ceased to con-duct herself with discretion, the happy moments that we experienced during the four or five years we were together in Gascony were no more.

Peace being restored, and my brother departed for France, as I have already relat-ed, the King my husband and I returned to Nerac. We were no sooner there than

Fosseuse persuaded the King my husband to make a journey to the waters of Aigues-Caudes, in Bearn, perhaps with a design to rid herself of her burden there. I begged the King my husband to excuse my accompanying him, as, since the affront that I had received at Pau, I had made a vow never to set foot in Bearn until the Catholic religion was reestablished there. He pressed me much to go with him, and grew angry at my persisting to refuse his request. He told me that his little girl (for so he affected to call Fosseuse) was desirous to go there on account of a colic, which she felt frequent returns of. I answered that I had no objection to his taking her with him. He then said that she could not go unless I went; that it would occasion scandal, which might as well be avoided. He continued to press me to accompany him, but at length I prevailed with him to consent to go without me, and to take her with him, and, with her, two of her companions, Rebours and Ville-Savin, together with the governess. They set out accordingly, and I waited their return at Baviere.

I had every day news from Rebours, informing me how matters went. This Rebours I have mentioned before to have been the object of my husband's passion, but she was now cast off, and, consequently, was no friend to Fosseuse, who had gained that place in his affection she had before held. She, therefore, strove all she could to circumvent her; and, indeed, she was fully qualified for such a purpose, as she was a cunning, deceitful young person. She gave me to understand that Fosseuse laboured to do me every ill office in her power; that she spoke of me with the greatest disrespect on all occasions, and expressed her expectations of marrying the King herself, in case she should be delivered of a son, when I was to be divorced. She had said, further, that when the King my husband returned to Baviere, he had resolved to go to Pau, and that I should go with him, whether I would or not.

This intelligence was far from being agreeable to me, and I knew not what to think of it. I trusted in the goodness of God, and I had a reliance on the generosity of the King my husband; yet I passed the time I waited for his return but uncomfortably, and often thought I shed more tears than they drank water. The Catholic nobility of the neighbourhood of Baviere used their utmost endeavours to divert my chagrin, for the month or five weeks that the King my husband and Fosseuse stayed at Aigues- Caudes.

On his return, a certain nobleman acquainted the King my husband with the concern I was under lest he should go to Pau, whereupon he did not press me on the subject, but only said he should have been glad if I had consented to go with him. Perceiving, by my tears and the expressions I made use of, that I should prefer even death to such a journey, he altered his intentions and we returned to Nerac.

The pregnancy of Fosseuse was now no longer a secret. The whole Court talked of it, and not only the Court, but all the country. I was willing to prevent the scandal from spreading, and accordingly resolved to talk to her on the subject. With this resolution, I took her into my closet, and spoke to her thus: "Though you have for some time estranged yourself from me, and, as it has been reported to me, striven to do me many ill offices with the King my husband, yet the regard I once had for you, and the esteem which I still entertain for those honourable persons to whose family you belong, do not admit of my neglecting to afford you all the assistance in my power in pour present unhappy situation. I beg you, there- fore, not to conceal the truth, it being both for your interest and mine, under whose protection you are, to declare it. Tell me the truth, and I will act towards you as a mother. You know that a contagious disorder has broken out in the place, and, under pretence of avoiding it, I will go to Mas-d'Agenois, which is a house belonging to the King my husband, in a very retired situation. I will take you with me, and such other persons as you shall name. Whilst we are there, the King will take the diversion of hunting in some other part of the country, and I shall not stir thence before your delivery. By this means we shall put a stop to the scan- dalous reports which are now current, and which concern yon more than myself."

So far from showing any contrition, or returning thanks for my kindness, she replied, with the utmost arrogance, that she would prove all those to be liars who had reported such things of her; that, for my part, I had ceased for a long time to show her any marks of regard, and she saw that I was determined upon her ruin. These words she delivered in as loud a tone as mine had been mildly expressed; and, leaving me abruptly, she flew in a rage to the King my husband, to relate to him what I had said to her. He was very angry upon the occasion, and declared he would make them all liars who had laid such things to her charge. From that moment until the hour of her delivery, which was a few months after, he never spoke to me.

She found the pains of labour come upon her about daybreak, whilst she was in bed in the chamber where the maids of honour slept. She sent for my physician, and begged him to go and acquaint the King my husband that she was taken ill. We slept in separate beds in the same chamber, and had done so for some time.

The physician delivered the message as he was directed, which greatly embar- rassed my husband. What to do he did not know. On the one hand, he was fear- ful of a discovery; on the other, he foresaw that, without proper assistance, there was danger of losing one he so much loved. In this dilemma, he resolved to apply to me, confess all, and implore my aid and advice, well knowing that, notwithstanding what had passed, I should be ready to do him a pleasure. Having come to this resolution, he withdrew my curtains, and spoke to me thus: "My dear, I have concealed a matter from you which I now confess. I beg you to forgive me, and to think no more about what I have said to you on the subject. Will you oblige me so far as to rise and go to Fosseuse, who is taken very ill? I am well assured that, in her present situation, you will forget everything and resent nothing. You know how dearly I love her, and I hope you will comply with my request." I answered that I had too great a respect for him to be offended at anything he should do, and that I would go to her immediately, and do as much for her as if she were a child of my own. I advised him, in the meantime, to go out and hunt, by which means he would draw away all his people, and prevent tattling.

I removed Fosseuse, with all convenient haste, from the chamber in which the maids of honour were, to one in a more retired part of the palace, got a physician and some women about her, and saw that she wanted for nothing that was proper in her situation. It pleased God that she should bring forth a daughter, since dead. As soon as she was delivered I ordered her to be taken back to the chamber from which she had been brought. Notwithstanding these precautions, it was not possible to prevent the story from circulating through the palace. When the King my husband returned from hunting he paid her a visit, according to custom. She begged that I might come and see her, as was usual with me when any one of my maids of honour was taken ill. By this means she expected to put a stop to stories to her prejudice. The King my husband came from her into my bedchamber, and found me in bed, as I was fatigued and required rest, after having been called up so early.

He begged me to get up and pay her a visit. I told him I went according to his desire before, when she stood in need of assistance, but now she wanted no help; that to visit her at this time would be only exposing her more, and cause myself to be pointed at by all the world. He seemed to be greatly displeased at what I said, which vexed me the more as I thought I did not deserve such treatment after what I had done at his request in the morning; she likewise contributed all in her power to aggravate matters betwixt him and me.

In the meantime, the King my brother, always well informed of what is passing in the families of the nobility of his kingdom, was not ignorant of the transactions of our Court. He was particularly curious to learn everything that happened with us, and knew every minute circumstance that I have now related. Thinking this a favourable occasion to wreak his vengeance on me for having been the means of my brother acquiring so much reputation by the peace he had brought about, he made use of the accident that happened in our Court to withdraw me from the King my husband, and thereby reduce me to the state of misery he wished to plunge me in. To this purpose he prevailed on the Queen my mother to write to me, and express her anxious desire to see me after an absence of five or six years. She added that a journey of this sort to Court would be serviceable to the affairs of the King my husband as well as my own; that the King my brother himself was desirous of seeing me, and that if I wanted money for the journey he would send it me. The King wrote to the same purpose, and despatched Manique, the steward of his household, with instructions to use every persuasion with me to undertake the journey. The length of time I had been absent in Gascony, and the unkind usage I received on account of Fosseuse, contributed to induce me to listen to the proposal made me.

The King and the Queen both wrote to me. I received three letters, in quick succession; and, that I might have no pretence for staying, I had the sum of fifteen hundred crowns paid me to defray the expenses of my journey. The Queen my mother wrote that she would give me the meeting in Saintonge, and that, if the King my husband would accompany me so far, she would treat with him there, and give him every satisfaction with respect to the King. But the King and she were desirous to have him at their Court, as he had been before with my brother; and the Marechal de Matignon had pressed the matter with the King, that he might have no one to interfere with him in Gascony. I had had too long experience of what was to be expected at their Court to hope much from all the fine promises that were made to me. I had resolved, however, to avail myself of the opportunity of an absence of a few months, thinking it might prove the means of setting matters to rights. Besides which, I thought that, as I should take Fosseuse with me, it was possible that the King's passion for her might cool when she was no longer in his sight, or he might attach himself to some other that was less inclined to do me mischief.

It was with some difficulty that the King my husband would consent to a removal, so unwilling was he to leave his Fosseuse. He paid more attention to me, in hopes that I should refuse to set out on this journey to France; but, as I had given my word in my letters to the King and the Queen my mother that I would go, and as I had even received money for the purpose, I could not do otherwise.

And herein my ill-fortune prevailed over the reluctance I had to leave the King my husband, after the instances of renewed love and regard which he had begun to show me.

# HISTORY OF THE HOUSE OF VALOIS.

CHARLES, COMTE DE VALOIS, was the younger brother of Philip the Fair, and therefore uncle of the three sovereigns lately dead. His eldest son Philip had been appointed guardian to the Queen of Charles IV.; and when it appeared that she had given birth to a daughter, and not a son, the barons, joining with the notables of Paris and the, good towns, met to decide who was by right the heir to the throne, "for the twelve peers of France said and say that the Crown of France is of such noble estate that by no succession can it come to a woman nor to a woman's son," as Froissart tells us. This being their view, the baby daughter of Charles IV. was at once set aside; and the claim of Edward III. of England, if, indeed, he ever made it, rested on Isabella of France, his mother, sister of the three sovereigns. And if succession through a female had been possible, then the daughters of those three kings had rights to be reserved. It was, however, clear that the throne must go to a man, and the crown was given to Philip of Valois, founder of a new house of sovereigns.

The new monarch was a very formidable person. He had been a great feudal lord, hot and vehement, after feudal fashion; but he was now to show that he could be a severe master, a terrible king. He began his reign by subduing the revolted Flemings on behalf of his cousin Louis of Flanders, and having replaced him in his dignities, returned to Paris and there held high state as King. And he clearly was a great sovereign; the weakness of the late King had not seriously injured France; the new King was the elect of the great lords, and they believed that his would be a new feudal monarchy; they were in the glow of their revenge over the Flemings for the days of Courtrai; his cousins reigned in Hungary and Naples, his sisters were married to the greatest of the lords; the Queen of Navarre was his cousin; even the youthful King of England did him homage for Guienne and

Ponthieu. The barons soon found out their mistake. Philip VI., supported by the lawyers, struck them whenever he gave them opening; he also dealt harshly with the traders, hampering them and all but ruining them, till the country was alarmed and discontented. On the other hand, young Edward of England had succeeded to a troubled inheritance, and at the beginning was far weaker than his rival; his own sagacity, and the advance of constitutional rights in England, soon enabled him to repair the breaches in his kingdom, and to gather fresh strength from the prosperity and good-will of a united people. While France followed a more restricted policy, England threw open her ports to all comers; trade grew in London as it waned in Paris; by his marriage with Philippa of Hainault, Edward secured a noble queen, and with her the happiness of his subjects and the all-important friendship of the Low Countries. In 1336 the followers of Philip VI. persuaded Louis of Flanders to arrest the English merchants then in Flanders; whereupon Edward retaliated by stopping the export of wool, and Jacquemart van Arteveldt of Ghent, then at the beginning of his power, persuaded the Flemish cities to throw off all allegiance to their French-loving Count, and to place themselves under the protection of Edward. In return Philip VI. put himself in communication with the Scots, the hereditary foes of England, and the great wars which were destined to last 116 years, and to exhaust the strength of two strong nations, were now about to begin. They brought brilliant and barren triumphs to England, and, like most wars, were a wasteful and terrible mistake, which, if crowned with ultimate success, might, by removing the centre of the kingdom into France, have marred the future welfare of England, for the happy constitutional development of the country could never have taken place with a sovereign living at Paris, and French interests becoming ever more powerful. Fortunately, therefore, while the war evoked by its brilliant successes the national pride of Englishmen, by its eventual failure it was prevented from inflicting permanent damage on England.

The war began in 1337 and ended in 1453; the epochs in it are the Treaty of Bretigny in 1360, the Treaty of Troyes in 1422, the final expulsion of the English in 1453.

The French King seems to have believed himself equal to the burdens of a great war, and able to carry out the most far-reaching plans. The Pope was entirely in his hands, and useful as a humble instrument to curb and harass the Emperor. Philip had proved himself master of the Flemish, and, with help of the King of Scotland, hoped so to embarrass Edward III. as to have no difficulty in eventually driving him to cede all his French possessions. While he thought it his interest to wear out his antagonist without any open fighting, it was Edward's interest to make vigorous and striking war. France therefore stood on the defensive; England was always the attacking party. On two sides, in Flanders and in Brittany, France had outposts which, if well defended, might long keep the English power away from her vitals. Unluckily for his side, Philip was harsh and raw, and threw these advantages away. In Flanders the repressive commercial policy of the Count, dictated from Paris, gave Edward the opportunity, in the end of 1337, of sending the Earl of Derby, with a strong fleet, to raise the blockade of Cadsand, and to open the Flemish markets by a brilliant action, in which the French chivalry was found powerless against the English yeoman-archers; and in 1338 Edward crossed over to Antwerp to see what forward movement could be made. The other frontier war was that of Brittany, which began a little later (1341). The openings of the war were gloomy and wasteful, without glory. Edward did not actually send defiance to Philip till 1339, when he proclaimed himself King of France, and quartered the lilies of France on the royal shield. The Flemish proved a very reed; and though the French army came up to meet the English in the Vermando country, no fighting took place, and the campaign of 1339 ended obscurely. Norman and Genoese ships threatened the southern shores of England, landing at Southampton and in the Isle of Wight unopposed. In 1340 Edward returned to Flanders; on his way he attacked the French fleet which lay at Sluys, and utterly destroyed it. The great victory of Sluys gave England for centuries the mastery of the British channel. But, important as it was, it gave no success to the land campaign. Edward wasted his strength on an unsuccessful siege of Tournia, and, ill-supported by his Flemish allies, could achieve nothing. The French King in this year seized on Guienne; and from Scotland tidings came that Edinburgh castle, the strongest place held by the English, had fallen into the hands of Douglas. Neither from Flanders nor from Guienne could Edward hope to reach the heart of the French power; a third inlet now presented itself in Brittany. On the death of John III. of Brittany, in 1341, Jean de Montfort, his youngest brother, claimed the great fief, against his niece Jeanne, daughter of his elder brother Guy, Comte de Penthievre. He urged that the Salic law, which had been recognised in the case of the crown, should also apply to this great duchy, so nearly an independent sovereignty. Jeanne had been married to Charles de Blois, whom John III. of Brittany had chosen as his heir; Charles was also nephew of King Philip, who gladly espoused his cause. Thereon Jean de Montfort appealed to Edward, and the two Kings met in border strife in Brittany. The Bretons sided with John against the influence of France. Both the claimants were made prisoners; the ladies carried on a chivalric warfare, Jeanne de Montfort against Jeanne de Blois, and all went favourably with the French party till Philip, with a barbarity as foolish as it was scandalous, tempted the chief Breton lords to Paris and beheaded them without trial. The war, suspended by a truce, broke out again, and the English raised large forces and supplies, meaning to attack on three sides at once,—from Flanders, Brittany, and Guienne. The Flemish expedition came to nothing; for the people of Ghent in

1345 murdered Jacques van Arteveldt as he was endeavouring to persuade them to receive the Prince of Wales as their count, and Edward, on learning this adverse news, returned to England. Thence, in July, 1346, he sailed for Normandy, and, landing at La Hogue, overran with ease the country up to Paris. He was not, however, strong enough to attack the capital, for Philip lay with a large army watching him at St. Denis. After a short hesitation Edward crossed the Seine at Poissy, and struck northwards, closely followed by Philip. He got across the Somme safely, and at Crecy in Ponthieu stood at bay to await the French. Though his numbers were far less than theirs, he had a good position, and his men were of good stuff; and when it came to battle, the defeat of the French was crushing. Philip had to fall back with his shattered army; Edward withdrew unmolested to Calais, which he took after a long siege in 1347. Philip had been obliged to call up his son John from the south, where he was observing the English under the Earl of Derby; thereupon the English overran all the south, taking Poitiers and finding no opposition. Queen Philippa of Hainault had also defeated and taken David of Scotland at Neville's Cross.

The campaign of 1346-1347 was on all hands disastrous to King Philip. He sued for and obtained a truce for ten months. These were the days of the "black death," which raged in France from 1347 to 1349, and completed the gloom of the country, vexed by an arbitrary and grasping monarch, by unsuccessful war, and now by the black cloud of pestilence. In 1350 King Philip died, leaving his crown to John of Normandy. He had added two districts and a title to France: he bought Montpellier from James of Aragon, and in 1349 also bought the territories of Humbert, Dauphin of Vienne, who resigned the world under influence of the revived religion of the time, a consequence of the plague, and became a Carmelite friar. The fief and the title of Dauphin were granted to Charles, the King's grandson, who was the first person who attached that title to the heir to the French throne. Apart from these small advantages, the kingdom of France had suffered terribly from the reign of the false and heartless Philip VI. Nor was France destined to enjoy better things under John "the Good," one of the worst sovereigns with whom she has been cursed. He took as his model and example the chivalric John of Bohemia, who had been one of the most extravagant and worthless of the princes of his time, and had perished in his old age at Crecy. The first act of the new King was to take from his kinsman, Charles "the Bad" of Navarre, Champagne and other lands; and Charles went over to the English King. King John was keen to fight; the States General gave him the means for carrying on war, by establishing the odious "gabelle" on salt, and other imposts. John hoped with his new army to drive the English completely out of the country. Petty war began again on all the frontiers,—an abortive attack on Calais, a guerilla warfare in Brittany, slight fighting also in Guienne. Edward in 1335 landed at Calais, but was recalled to pacify Scotland; Charles of Navarre and the Duke of Lancaster were on the Breton border; the Black Prince sailed for Bordeaux. In 1356 he rode northward with a small army to the Loire, and King John, hastily summoning all his nobles and fief-holders, set out to meet him. Hereon the Black Prince, whose forces were weak, began to retreat; but the French King outmarched and intercepted him near Poitiers. He had the English completely in his power, and with a little patience could have starved them into submission; instead, he deemed it his chivalric duty to avenge Crecy in arms, and the great battle of Poitiers was the result (19th September, 1356). The carnage and utter ruin of the French feudal army was quite incredible; the dead seemed more than the whole army of the Black Prince; the prisoners were too many to be held. The French army, bereft of leaders, melted away, and the Black Prince rode triumphantly back to Bordeaux with the captive King John and his brave little son in his train. A two years' truce ensued; King John was carried over to London, where he found a fellow in misfortune in David of Scotland, who had been for eleven years a captive in English hands. The utter degradation of the nobles, and the misery of the country, gave to the cities of France an opportunity which one great man, Etienne Marcel, provost of the traders at Paris, was not slow to grasp. He fortified the capital and armed the citizens; the civic clergy made common cause with him; and when the Dauphin Charles convoked the three Estates at Paris, it was soon seen that the nobles had become completely discredited and powerless. It was a moment in which a new life might have begun for France; in vain did the noble order clamour for war and taxes,—they to do the war, with what skill and success all men now knew, and the others to pay the taxes. Clergy, however, and burghers resisted. The Estates parted, leaving what power there was still in France in the hands of Etienne Marcel. He strove in vain to reconcile Charles the Dauphin with Charles of Navarre, who stood forward as a champion of the towns. Very reluctantly did Marcel entrust his fortunes to such hands. With help of Lecocq, Bishop of Laon, he called the Estates again together, and endeavoured to lay down sound principles of government, which Charles the Dauphin was compelled to accept. Paris, however, stood alone, and even there all were not agreed. Marcel and Bishop Lecocq, seeing the critical state of things, obtained the release of Charles of Navarre, then a prisoner. The result was that ere long the Dauphin-regent was at open war with Navarre and with Paris. The outbreak of the miserable peasantry, the Jacquerie, who fought partly for revenge against the nobles, partly to help Paris, darkened the time; they were repressed with savage bloodshed, and in 1358 the Dauphin's party in Paris assassinated the only great man France had seen for long. With Etienne Marcel's death all hope of a constitutional life died out from France; the Dauphin entered Paris and set his foot on the conquered liberties of his country. Paris had stood almost alone; civic strength is wanting in France; the towns but feebly supported Marcel; they compelled the movement to lose its popular and general character, and to become a first attempt to govern France from Paris alone. After some insincere negotiations, and a fear of desultory warfare, in which Edward III. traversed France without meeting with a single foe to fight, peace was at last agreed to, at Bretigny, in May, 1360. By this act Edward III. renounced the French throne and gave up all he claimed or held north of the Loire, while he was secured in the lordship of the south and west, as well as that part of Northern Picardy which included Calais, Guines, and Ponthieu. The treaty also fixed the ransom to be paid by King John.

France was left smaller than she had been under Philip Augustus, yet she received this treaty with infinite thankfulness; worn out with war and weakness, any diminution of territory seemed better to her than a continuance of her unbearable misfortunes. Under Charles, first as Regent, then as King, she enjoyed an uneasy rest and peace for twenty years.

King John, after returning for a brief space to France, went back into his pleasant captivity in England, leaving his country to be ruled by the Regent the Dauphin. In 1364 he died, and Charles V., "the Wise," became King in name, as he had now been for some years in fact. This cold, prudent, sickly prince, a scholar who laid the foundations of the great library in Paris by placing 900 MSS. in three chambers in the Louvre, had nothing to dazzle the ordinary eye; to the timid spirits of that age he seemed to be a malevolent wizard, and his name of "Wise" had in it more of fear than of love. He also is notable for two things: he reformed the current coin, and recognised the real worth of Du Guesclin, the first great leader of mercenaries in France, a grim fighting-man, hostile to the show of feudal warfare, and herald of a new age of contests, in which the feudal levies would fall into the background. The invention of gunpowder in this century, the incapacity of the great lords, the rise of free lances and mercenary troops, all told that a new era had arrived. It was by the hand of Du Guesclin that Charles overcame his cousin and namesake, Charles of Navarre, and compelled him to peace. On the other hand, in the Breton war which followed just after, he was defeated by Sir John Chandos and the partisans of Jean de Montfort, who made him prisoner; the Treaty of Guerande, which followed, gave them the dukedom of Brittany; and Charles V., unable to resist, was fair to receive the new duke's homage, and to confirm him in the duchy. The King did not rest till he had ransomed Du Guesclin from the hands of Chandos; he then gave him commission to raise a paid army of freebooters, the scourge of France, and to march with them to support, against the Black Prince, the claims of Henry of Trastamare to the Crown of Castile. Successful at first by help of the King of Aragon, he was made Constable of Spain at the coronation of Henry at Burgos. Edward the Black Prince, however, intervened, and at the battle of Najara (1367) Du Guesclin was again a prisoner in

English hands, and Henry lost his throne. Fever destroyed the victorious host, and the Black Prince, withdrawing into Gascony, carried with him the seeds of the disorder which shortened his days. Du Guesclin soon got his liberty again; and Charles V., seeing how much his great rival of England was weakened, determined at last on open war. He allied himself with Henry of Trastamare, listened to the grievances of the Aquitanians, summoned the Black Prince to appear and answer the complaints. In 1369, Henry defeated Pedro, took him prisoner, and murdered him in a brawl; thus perished the hopes of the English party in the south. About the same time Charles V. sent open defiance and declaration of war to England. Without delay, he surprised the English in the north, recovering all Ponthieu at once; the national pride was aroused; Philip, Duke of Burgundy, who had, through the prudent help of Charles, lately won as a bride the heiress of Flanders, was stationed at Rouen, to cover the western approach to Paris, with strict orders not to fight; the Aquitanians were more than half French at heart. The record of the war is as the smoke of a furnace. We see the reek of burnt and plundered towns; there were no brilliant feats of arms; the Black Prince, gloomy and sick, abandoned the struggle, and returned to England to die; the new governor, the Earl of Pembroke, did not even succeed in landing: he was attacked and defeated off Rochelle by Henry of Castile, his whole fleet, with all its treasure and stores, taken or sunk, and he himself was a prisoner in Henry's hands. Du Guesclin had already driven the English out of the west into Brittany; he now overran Poitou, which received him gladly; all the south seemed to be at his feet. The attempt of Edward III. to relieve the little that remained to him in France failed utterly, and by 1372 Poitou was finally lost to England. Charles set himself to reduce Brittany with considerable success; a diversion from Calais caused plentiful misery in the open country; but, as the French again refused to fight, it did nothing to restore the English cause. By 1375 England held nothing in France except Calais, Cherbourg, Bayonne, and Bordeaux. Edward III., utterly worn out with war, agreed to a truce, through intervention of the Pope; it was signed in 1375. In 1377, on its expiring, Charles, who in two years had sedulously improved the state of France, renewed the war. By sea and land the English were utterly overmatched, and by 1378 Charles was master of the situation on all hands. Now, however, he pushed his advantages too far; and the cold skill which had overthrown the English, was used in vain against the Bretons, whose duchy he desired to absorb. Languedoc and Flanders also revolted against him. France was heavily burdened with taxes, and the future was dark and threatening. In the midst of these things, death overtook the coldly calculating monarch in September, 1380.

Little had France to hope from the boy who was now called on to fill the throne. Charles VI. was not twelve years old, a light-wined, handsome boy, under the guardianship of the royal Dukes his uncles, who had no principles except that of their own interest to guide them in bringing up the King and ruling the people. Before Charles VI. had reached years of discretion, he was involved by the French nobles in war against the Flemish cities, which, under guidance of the great Philip van Arteveldt, had overthrown the authority of the Count of Flanders. The French cities showed ominous signs of being inclined to ally themselves with the civic movement in the north. The men of Ghent came out to meet their French foes, and at the battle of Roosebek (1382) were utterly defeated and crushed. Philip van Arteveldt himself was slain. It was a great triumph of the nobles over the cities; and Paris felt it when the King returned. All movement there and in the other northern cities of France was ruthlessly repressed; the noble reaction also overthrew the "new men" and the lawyers, by whose means the late King had chiefly governed. Two years later, the royal Dukes signed a truce with England, including Ghent in it; and Louis de Male, Count of Flanders, having perished at the same time, Marguerite his daughter, wife of Philip of Burgundy, succeeded to his inheritance (1384.) Thus began the high fortunes of the House of Burgundy, which at one time seemed to overshadow Emperor and King of France. In 1385, another of the brothers, Louis, Duc d'Anjou, died, with all his Italian ambitions unfulfilled. In 1386, Charles VI., under guidance of his uncles, declared war on England, and exhausted all France in preparations; the attempt proved the sorriest failure. The regency of the Dukes became daily more unpopular, until in 1388 Charles dismissed his two uncles, the Dukes of Burgundy and Berri, and began to rule. For a while all went much better; he recalled his father's friends and advisers, lightened the burdens of the people, allowed the new ministers free hand in making prudent government; and learning how bad had been the state of the south under the Duc de Berri, deprived him of that command in 1390. Men thought that the young King, if not good himself, was well content to allow good men to govern in his name; at any, rate, the rule of the selfish Dukes seemed to be over. Their bad influences, however, still surrounded him; an attempt to assassinate Olivier de Clisson, the Constable, was connected with their intrigues and those of the Duke of Brittany; and in setting forth to punish the attempt on his favourite the Constable, the unlucky young King, who had sapped his health by debauchery, suddenly became mad. The Dukes of Burgundy and Berri at once seized the reins and put aside his brother the young Duc d'Orleans. It was the beginning of that great civil discord between Burgundy and Orleans, the Burgundians and Armagnacs, which worked so much ill for France in the earlier part of the next century. The rule of the uncles was disastrous for France; no good government seemed even possible for that unhappy land.

An obscure strife went on until 1404, when Duke Philip of Burgundy died, leaving his vast inheritance to John the Fearless, the deadly foe of Louis d'Orleans. Paris was with him, as with his father before him; the Duke entered the capital in

1405, and issued a popular proclamation against the ill-government of the Queen-regent and Orleans. Much profession of a desire for better things was made, with small results. So things went on until 1407, when, after the Duc de Berri, who tried to play the part of a mediator, had brought the two Princes together, the Duc d'Orleans was foully assassinated by a Burgundian partisan. The Duke of Burgundy, though he at first withdrew from Paris, speedily returned, avowed the act, and was received with plaudits by the mob. For a few years the strife continued, obscure and bad; a great league of French princes and nobles was made to stem the success of the Burgundians; and it was about this time that the Armagnac name became common. Paris, however, dominated by the "Cabochians," the butchers' party, the party of the "marrowbones and cleavers," and entirely devoted to the Burgundians, enabled John the Fearless to hold his own in France; the King himself seemed favourable to the same party. In 1412 the princes were obliged to come to terms, and the Burgundian triumph seemed complete. In 1413 the wheel went round, and we find the Armagnacs in Paris, rudely sweeping away all the Cabochians with their professions of good civic rule. The Duc de Berri was made captain of Paris, and for a while all went against the Burgundians, until, in 1414, Duke John was fain to make the first Peace of Arras, and to confess himself worsted in the strife. The young Dauphin Louis took the nominal lead of the national party, and ruled supreme in Paris in great ease and self-indulgence.

The year before, Henry V. had succeeded to the throne of England,—a bright and vigorous young man, eager to be stirring in the world, brave and fearless, with a stern grasp of things beneath all,—a very sheet- anchor of firmness and determined character. Almost at the very opening of his reign, the moment he had secured his throne, he began a negotiation with France which boded no good. He offered to marry Catharine, the King's third daughter, and therewith to renew the old Treaty of Bretigny, if her dower were Normandy, Maine, Anjou, not without a good sum of money. The French Court, on the other hand, offered him her hand with Aquitaine and the money, an offer rejected instantly; and Henry made ready for a rough wooing in arms. In 1415 he crossed to Harfleur, and while parties still fought in France, after a long and exhausting siege, took the place; thence he rode northward for Calais, feeling his army too much reduced to attempt more. The Armagnacs, who had gathered at Rouen, also pushed fast to the north, and having choice of passage over the Somme, Amiens being in their hands, got before King Henry, while he had to make a long round before he could get across that stream. Consequently, when, on his way, he reached Azincourt, he found the whole chivalry of France arrayed against him in his path. The great battle of Azincourt followed, with frightful ruin and carnage of the French. With a huge crowd of prisoners the young King passed on to Calais, and thence to England.

The Armagnacs' party lay buried in the hasty graves of Azincourt; never had there been such slaughter of nobles. Still, for three years they made head against their foes; till in 1418 the Duke of Burgundy's friends opened Paris's gates to his soldiers, and for the time the Armagnacs seemed to be completely defeated; only the Dauphin Charles made feeble war from Poitiers. Henry V. with a fresh army had already made another descent on the Normandy coast; the Dukes of Anjou, Brittany, and Burgundy made several and independent treaties with him; and it seemed as though France had completely fallen in pieces. Henry took Rouen, and although the common peril had somewhat silenced the strife of faction, no steps were taken to meet him or check his course; on the contrary, matters were made even more hopeless by the murder of John, Duke of Burgundy, in 1419, even as he was kneeling and offering reconciliation at the young Dauphin's feet. The young Duke, Philip, now drew at once towards Henry, whom his father had apparently wished with sincerity to check; Paris, too, was weary of the Armagnac struggle, and desired to welcome Henry of England; the Queen of France also went over to the Anglo-Burgundian side. The end of it was that on May 21,1420, was signed the famous Treaty of Troyes, which secured the Crown of France to Henry, by the exclusion of the Dauphin Charles, whenever poor mad Charles VI., should cease to live. Meanwhile, Henry was made Regent of France, promising to maintain all rights and privileges of the Parliament and nobles, and to crush the Dauphin with his Armagnac friends, in token whereof he was at once wedded to Catharine of France, and set forth to quell the opposition of the provinces. By Christmas all France north of the Loire was in English hands. All the lands to the south of the river remained firmly fixed in their allegiance to the Dauphin and the Armagnacs, and these began to feel themselves to be the true French party, as opposed to the foreign rule of the English. For barely two years that rule was carried on by Henry V. with inflexible justice, and Northern France saw with amazement the presence of a real king, and an orderly government. In 1422 King Henry died; a few weeks later Charles VI. died also, and the face of affairs began to change, although, at the first, Charles VII. the "Well-served," the lazy, listless prince, seemed to have little heart for the perils and efforts of his position. He was proclaimed King at Mehun, in Berri, for the true France for the time lay on that side of the Loire, and the Regent Bedford, who took the reins at Paris, was a vigorous and powerful prince, who was not likely to give way to an idle dreamer. At the outset Charles suffered two defeats, at Crevant in 1423, and at Verneuil in 1424, and things seemed to be come to their worst. Yet he was prudent, conciliatory, and willing to wait; and as the English power in France—that triangle of which the base was the sea-line from Harfleur to Calais, and the apex Paris—was unnatural and far from being really strong; and as the relations between Bedford and Burgundy might not always be friendly, the man who could wait had many chances in his favour. Before long, things began to mend; Charles wedded Marie d'Anjou, and won over that great house to the French side; more and more was he regarded as the nation's King; symptoms of a wish for reconciliation with Burgundy appeared; the most vehement Armagnacs were sent away from Court. Causes of disagreement also shook the friendship between Burgundy and England.

Feeling the evils of inaction most, Bedford in 1428 decided on a forward movement, and sent the Earl of Salisbury to the south. He first secured his position on the north of the Loire, then, crossing that river, laid siege to Orleans, the key to the south, and the last bulwark of the national party. All efforts to vex or dislodge him failed; and the attempt early in 1429 to stop the English supplies was completely defeated at Bouvray; from the salt fish captured, the battle has taken the name of "the Day of the Herrings." Dunois, Bastard of Orleans, was, wounded; the Scots, the King's body-guard, on whom fell ever the grimmest of the fighting, suffered terribly, and their leader was killed. All went well for Bedford till it suited the Duke of Burgundy to withdraw from his side, carrying with him a large part of the fighting power of the besiegers. Things were already looking rather gloomy in the English camp, when a new and unexpected rumour struck all hearts cold with fear. A virgin, an Amazon, had been raised up as a deliverer for France, and would soon be on them, armed with mysterious powers.

A young peasant girl, one Jeanne d'Arc, had been brought up in the village of Domremy, hard by the Lorraine border. The district, always French in feeling, had lately suffered much from Burgundian raids; and this young damsel, brooding over the treatment of her village and her country, and filled with that strange vision-power which is no rare phenomenon in itself with young girls, came at last to believe with warm and active faith in heavenly appearances and messages, all urging her to deliver France and her King. From faith to action the bridge is short; and ere long the young dreamer of seventeen set forth to work her miracle. Her history is quite unique in the world; and though probably France would ere many years have shaken off the English yoke, for its strength was rapidly going, still to her is the credit of having proved its weakness, and of having asserted the triumphant power of a great belief. All gave way before her; Charles VII., persuaded doubtless by his mother-in-law, Yolande of Aragon, who warmly espoused her cause, listened readily to the maiden's voice; and as that voice urged only what was noble and pure, she carried conviction as she went. In the end she received the King's commission to undertake the relief of Orleans. Her coming was fresh blood to the defence; a new spirit seemed to be poured out on all her followers, and in like manner a deep dejection settled down on the English. The blockade was forced, and, in eight days the besiegers raised the siege and marched away. They withdrew to Jargeau, where they were attacked and routed with great loss.

A little later Talbot himself, who had marched to help them, was also defeated and taken. Then, compelling Charles to come out from his in glorious ease, she carried him triumphantly with her to Rheims, where he was duly crowned King, the Maid of Orléans standing by, and holding aloft the royal standard. She would gladly have gone home to Domremy now, her mission being accomplished; for she was entirely free from all ambitious or secondary aims. But she was too great a power to be spared. Northern France was still in English hands, and till the English were cast out her work was not complete; so they made her stay, sweet child, to do the work which, had there been any manliness in them, they ought to have found it easy to achieve for themselves. The dread of her went before her,—a pillar of cloud and darkness to the English, but light and hope to her countrymen. Men believed that she was called of God to regenerate the world, to destroy the Saracen at last, to bring in the millennial age. Her statue was set up in the churches, and crowds prayed before her image as before a popular saint.

The incapacity and ill-faith of those round the King gave the English some time to recover themselves; Bedford and Burgundy drew together again, and steps were taken to secure Paris. When, however, Jeanne, weary of courtly delays, marched, contemptuous of the King, as far as St. Denis, friends sprang up on every side. In Normandy, on the English line of communications, four strong places were surprised; and Bedford, made timid as to his supplies, fell back to Rouen, leaving only a small garrison in Paris. Jeanne, ill-supported by the royal troops, failed in her attack on the city walls, and was made prisoner by the Burgundians; they handed her over to the English, and she was, after previous indignities, and such treatment as chivalry alone could have dealt her, condemned as a witch, and burnt as a relapsed heretic at Rouen in 1431. Betrayed by the French Court, sold by the Burgundians, murdered by the English, unrescued by the people of France which she so much loved, Jeanne d'Arc died the martyr's death, a pious, simple soul, a heroine of the purest metal. She saved her country, for the English power never recovered from the shock. The churchmen who burnt her, the Frenchmen of the unpatriotic party, would have been amazed could they have foreseen that nearly 450 years afterwards, churchmen again would glorify her name as the saint of the Church, in opposition to both the religious liberties and the national feelings of her country.

The war, after having greatly weakened the noblesse, and having caused infinite sufferings to France, now drew towards a close; the Duke of Burgundy at last agreed to abandon his English allies, and at a great congress at Arras, in 1435, signed a treaty with Charles VII. by which he solemnly came over to the French side. On condition that he should get Auxerre and Macon, as well as the towns on and near the river Somme, he was willing to recognise Charles as King of

France. His price was high, yet it was worth all that was given; for, after all, he was of the French blood royal, and not a foreigner. The death of Bedford, which took place about the same time, was almost a more terrible blow to the fortunes of the English. Paris opened her gates to her King in April, 1436; the long war kept on with slight movements now and then for several years.

The next year was marked by the meeting of the States General, and the establishment, in principle at least, of a standing army. The Estates petitioned the willing King that the system of finance in the realm should be remodelled, and a permanent tax established for the support of an army. Thus, it was thought, solidity would be given to the royal power, and the long-standing curse of the freebooters and brigands cleared away. No sooner was this done than the nobles began to chafe under it; they scented in the air the coming troubles; they, took as their head, poor innocents, the young Dauphin Louis, who was willing enough to resist the concentration of power in royal hands. Their champion of 1439, the leader of the "Praguerie," as this new league was called, in imitation, it is said, of the Hussite movement at Prague, the enthusiastic defender of noble privilege against the royal power, was the man who afterwards, as Louis XI., was the destroyer of the noblesse on behalf of royalty. Some of the nobles stood firmly by the King, and, aided by them and by an army of paid soldiers serving under the new conditions, Charles VII., no contemptible antagonist when once aroused, attacked and overthrew the Praguerie; the cities and the country people would have none of it; they preferred peace under a king's strong hand. Louis was sent down to the east to govern Dauphiny; the lessons of the civil war were not lost on Charles; he crushed the freebooters of Champagne, drove the English out of Pontois in 1441, moved actively up and down France, reducing anarchy, restoring order, resisting English attacks. In the last he was loyally supported by the Dauphin, who was glad to find a field for his restless temper. He repulsed the English at Dieppe, and put down the Comte d'Armagnac in the south. During the two years' truce with England which now followed, Charles VII. and Louis drew off their free-lances eastward, and the Dauphin came into rude collision with the Swiss not far from Basel, in 1444. Some sixteen hundred mountaineers long and heroically withstood at St. Jacob the attack of several thousand Frenchmen, fighting stubbornly till they all perished.

The King and Dauphin returned to Paris, having defended their border- lands with credit, and having much reduced the numbers of the lawless free-lances. The Dauphin, discontented again, was obliged once more to withdraw into Dauphiny, where he governed prudently and with activity. In 1449, the last scene of the Anglo-French war began. In that year English adventurers landed on the Breton coast; the Duke called the French King to his aid. Charles did not tarry this time;

he broke the truce with England; he sent Dunois into Normandy, and himself soon followed. In both duchies, Brittany and Normandy, the French were welcomed with delight: no love for England lingered in the west. Somerset and Talbot failed to defend Rouen, and were driven from point to point, till every stronghold was lost to them. Dunois then passed into Guienne, and in a few months Bayonne, the last stronghold of the English, fell into his hands (1451). When Talbot was sent over to Bordeaux with five thousand men to recover the south, the old English feeling revived, for England was their best customer, and they had little in common with France. It was, however, but a last flicker of the flame; in July, 1453, at the siege of Castillon, the aged Talbot was slain and the war at once came to an end; the south passed finally into the kingdom of France. Normandy and Guienne were assimilated to France in taxation and army organisation; and all that remained to England across the Channel was Calais, with Havre and Guines Castle. Her foreign ambitions and struggles over, England was left to consume herself in civil strife, while France might rest and recover from the terrible sufferings she had undergone. The state of the country had become utterly wretched.

With the end of the English wars new life began to gleam out on France; the people grew more tranquil, finding that toil and thrift bore again their wholesome fruits; Charles VII. did not fail in his duty, and took his part in restoring quiet, order, and justice in the land.

The French Crown, though it had beaten back the English, was still closely girt in with rival neighbours, the great dukes on every frontier. All round the east and north lay the lands of Philip of Burgundy; to the west was the Duke of Brittany, cherishing a jealous independence; the royal Dukes, Berri, Bourbon, Anjou, are all so many potential sources of danger and difficulty to the Crown. The conditions of the nobility are altogether changed; the old barons have sunk into insignificance; the struggle of the future will lie between the King's cousins and himself, rather than with the older lords. A few non-royal princes, such as Armagnac, or Saint-Pol, or Brittany, remain and will go down with the others; the "new men" of the day, the bastard Dunois or the Constables Du Guesclin and Clisson, grow to greater prominence; it is clear that the old feudalism is giving place to a newer order, in which the aristocracy, from the King's brothers downwards, will group themselves around the throne, and begin the process which reaches its unhappy perfection under Louis XIV.

Directly after the expulsion of the English, troubles began between King Charles VII. and the Dauphin Louis; the latter could not brook a quiet life in Dauphiny, and the King refused him that larger sphere in the government of Normandy which he coveted. Against his father's will, Louis married Charlotte of Savoy, daughter of his strongest neighbour in Dauphiny; suspicion and bad feeling grew strong between father and son; Louis was specially afraid of his father's counsellors; the King was specially afraid of his son's craftiness and ambition. It came to an open rupture, and Louis, in 1456, fled to the Court of Duke Philip of Burgundy. There he lived at refuge at Geneppe, meddling a good deal in Burgundian politics, and already opposing himself to his great rival, Charles of Charolais, afterwards Charles the Bold, the last Duke of Burgundy. Bickerings, under his bad influence, took place between King and Duke; they never burst out into flame. So things went on uncomfortably enough, till Charles VII. died in 1461 and the reign of Louis XI. began.

Between father and son what contrast could be greater? Charles VII., "the Well-served," so easygoing, so open and free from guile; Louis XI., so shy of counsellors, so energetic and untiring, so close and guileful. History does but apologise for Charles, and even when she fears and dislikes Louis, she cannot forbear to wonder and admire. And yet Louis enslaved his country, while Charles had seen it rescued from foreign rule; Charles restored something of its prosperity, while Louis spent his life in crushing its institutions and in destroying its elements of independence. A great and terrible prince, Louis XI. failed in having little or no constructive power; he was strong to throw down the older society, he built little in its room. Most serious of all was his action with respect to the district of the River Somme, at that time the northern frontier of France. The towns there had been handed over to Philip of Burgundy by the Treaty of Arras, with a stipulation that the Crown might ransom them at any time, and this Louis succeeded in doing in 1463. The act was quite blameless and patriotic in itself, yet it was exceedingly unwise, for it thoroughly alienated Charles the Bold, and led to the wars of the earlier period of the reign. Lastly, as if he had not done enough to offend the nobles, Louis in 1464 attacked their hunting rights, touching them in their tenderest part. No wonder that this year saw the formation of a great league against him, and the outbreak of a dangerous civil war. The "League of the Public Weal" was nominally headed by his own brother Charles, heir to the throne; it was joined by Charles of Charolais, who had completely taken the command of affairs in the Burgundian territories, his father the old duke being too feeble to withstand him; the Dukes of Brittany, Nemours, Bourbon, John of Anjou, Duke of Calabria, the Comte d'Armagnac, the aged Dunois, and a host of other princes and nobles flocked in; and the King had scarcely any forces at his back with which to withstand them. His plans for the campaign against the league were admirable, though they were frustrated by the bad faith of his captains, who mostly sympathised with this outbreak of the feudal nobility. Louis himself marched southward to quell the Duc de Bourbon and his friends, and returning from that task, only half done for lack of time, he found that Charles of Charolais had passed by Paris, which was faithful to the King, and was coming down southwards, intending to join the Dukes of Berri and Brittany, who were on their way towards the capital. The hostile armies met at Montleheri on the Orleans road; and after a strange battle—minutely described by Commines—a battle in which both sides ran away, and neither ventured at first to claim a victory, the King withdrew to Corbeil, and then marched into Paris (1465). There the armies of the league closed in on him; and after a siege of several weeks, Louis, feeling disaffection all around him, and doubtful how long Paris herself would bear for him the burdens of blockade, signed the Peace of Conflans, which, to all appearances, secured the complete victory to the noblesse, "each man carrying off his piece." Instantly the contented princes broke up their half-starved armies and went home, leaving Louis behind to plot and contrive against them, a far wiser man, thanks to the lesson they had taught him. They did not let him wait long for a chance. The Treaty of Conflans had given the duchy of Normandy to the King's brother Charles; he speedily quarrelled with his neighbour, the Duke of Brittany, and Louis came down at once into Normandy, which threw itself into his arms, and the whole work of the league was broken up. The Comte de Charolais, occupied with revolts at Dinan and Liege, could not interfere, and presently his father, the old Duke Philip, died (1467), leaving to him the vast lordships of the House of Burgundy.

And now the "imperial dreamer," Charles the Bold, was brought into immediate rivalry with that royal trickster, the "universal spider," Louis XI. Charles was by far the nobler spirit of the two: his vigour and intelligence, his industry and wish to raise all around him to a higher cultivation, his wise reforms at home, and attempts to render his father's dissolute and careless rule into a well-ordered lordship, all these things marked him out as the leading spirit of the time. His territories were partly held under France, partly under the empire: the Artois district, which also may be taken to include the Somme towns, the county of Rhetel, the duchy of Bar, the duchy of Burgundy, with Auxerre and Nevers, were feudally in France; the rest of his lands under the empire. He had, therefore, interests and means of interference on either hand; and it is clear that Charles set before himself two different lines of policy, according as he looked one way or the other.

At the time of Duke Philip's death a new league had been formed against Louis, embracing the King of England, Edward IV., the Dukes of Burgundy and Brittany, and the Kings of Aragon and Castile. Louis strained every nerve, he conciliated Paris, struck hard at disaffected partisans, and in 1468 convoked the States General at Tours. The three Estates were asked to give an opinion as to the power of the Crown to alienate Normandy, the step insisted upon by the Duke of Burgundy. Their reply was to the effect that the nation forbids the Crown to dismember the realm; they supported their opinion by liberal promises of help. Thus fortified by the sympathy of his people, Louis began to break up the coalition. He made terms with the Duc de Bourbon and the House of Anjou; his brother Charles was a cipher; the King of England was paralysed by the antagonism of Warwick; he attacked and reduced Brittany; Burgundy, the most formidable, alone remained to be dealt with. How should he meet him?— by war or by negotiation? His Court was divided in opinion; the King decided for himself in favour of the way of negotiation, and came to the astonishing conclusion that he would go and meet the Duke and win him over to friendship. He miscalculated both his own powers of persuasion and the force of his antagonist's temper. The interview of Peronne followed; Charles held his visitor as a captive, and in the end compelled him to sign a treaty, of peace, on the basis of that of Conflans, which had closed the War of the Public Weal. And as if this were not sufficient humiliation, Charles made the King accompany him on his expedition to punish the men of Liege, who, trusting to the help of Louis, had again revolted (1469). This done, he allowed the degraded monarch to return home to Paris. An assembly of notables of Tours speedily declared the Treaty of Perrone null, and the King made some small frontier war on the Duke, which was ended by a truce at Amiens, in 1471. The truce was spent in preparation for a fresh struggle, which Louis, to whom time was everything, succeeded in deferring from point to point, till the death of his brother Charles, now Duc de Guienne, in 1472, broke up the formidable combination. Charles the Bold at once broke truce and made war on the King, marching into northern France, sacking towns and ravaging the country, till he reached Beauvais. There the despair of the citizens and the bravery of the women saved the town. Charles raised the siege and marched on Rouen, hoping to meet the Duke of Brittany; but that Prince had his hands full, for Louis had overrun his territories, and had reduced him to terms. The Duke of Burgundy saw that the coalition had completely failed; he too made fresh truce with Louis at Senlis (1472), and only, deferred, he no doubt thought, the direct attack on his dangerous rival. Henceforth Charles the Bold turned his attention mainly to the east, and Louis gladly saw him go forth to spend his strength on distant ventures; saw the interview at Treves with the Emperor Frederick III., at which the Duke's plans were foiled by the suspicions of the Germans and the King's intrigues; saw the long siege of the Neusz wearing out his power; bought off the hostility of Edward IV. of England, who had undertaken to march on Paris; saw Charles embark on his Swiss enterprise; saw the subjugation of Lorraine and capture of Nancy (1475), the battle of Granson, the still more fatal defeat of Morat (1476), and lastly the final struggle of Nancy, and the Duke's death on the field (January, 1477).

While Duke Charles had thus been running on his fate, Louis XI. had actively attacked the larger nobles of France, and had either reduced them to submission or had destroyed them.

As Duke Charles had left no male heir, the King at once resumed the duchy of Burgundy, as a male fief of the kingdom; he also took possession of Franche Comte at the same time; the King's armies recovered all Picardy, and even entered Flanders. Then Mary of Burgundy, hoping to raise up a barrier against this dangerous neighbour, offered her hand, with all her great territories, to young Maximilian of Austria, and married him within six months after her father's death. To this wedding is due the rise to real greatness of the House of Austria; it begins the era of the larger politics of modern times.

After a little hesitation Louis determined to continue the struggle against the Burgundian power. He secured Franche Comte, and on his northern frontier retook Arras, that troublesome border city, the "bonny Carlisle" of those days; and advancing to relieve Therouenne, then besieged by Maximilian, fought and lost the battle of Guinegate (1479). The war was languid after this; a truce followed in 1480, and a time of quiet for France. Charles the Dauphin was engaged to marry the little Margaret, Maximilian's daughter, and as her dower she was to bring Franche Comte and sundry places on the border line disputed between the two princes. In these last days Louis XI. shut himself up in gloomy seclusion in his castle of Plessis near Tours, and there he died in 1483. A great king and a terrible one, he has left an indelible mark on the history of France, for he was the founder of France in its later form, as an absolute monarchy ruled with little regard to its own true welfare. He had crushed all resistance; he had enlarged the borders of France, till the kingdom took nearly its modern dimensions; he had organised its army and administration. The danger was lest in the hands of a feeble boy these great results should be squandered away, and the old anarchy once more raise its head.

For Charles VIII., who now succeeded, was but thirteen years old, a weak boy whom his father had entirely neglected, the training of his son not appearing to be an essential part of his work in life. The young Prince had amused himself with romances, but had learnt nothing useful. A head, however, was found for him in the person of his eldest sister Anne, whom Louis XI. had married to Peter II., Lord of Beaujeu and Duc de Bourbon. To her the dying King entrusted the guardianship of his son; and for more than nine years Anne of France was virtual King. For those years all went well.

With her disappearance from the scene, the controlling hand is lost, and France begins the age of her Italian expeditions.

When the House of Anjou came to an end in 1481, and Anjou and Maine fell in to the Crown, there fell in also a far less valuable piece of property, the claim of that house descended from Charles, the youngest brother of Saint Louis, on the kingdom of Naples and Sicily. There was much to tempt an ambitious prince in the state of Italy. Savoy, which held the passage into the peninsula, was then thoroughly French in sympathy; Milan, under Lodovico Sforza, "il Moro," was in alliance with Charles; Genoa preferred the French to the Aragonese claimants for influence over Italy; the popular feeling in the cities, especially in Florence, was opposed to the despotism of the Medici, and turned to France for deliverance; the misrule of the Spanish Kings of Naples had made Naples thoroughly discontented; Venice was, as of old, the friend of France. Tempted by these reasons, in 1494 Charles VIII. set forth for Italy with a splendid host. He displayed before the eyes of Europe the first example of a modern army, in its three well-balanced branches of infantry, cavalry, and artillery. There was nothing in Italy to withstand his onslaught; he swept through the land in triumph; Charles believed himself to be a great conqueror giving law to admiring subject- lands; he entered Pisa, Florence, Rome itself. Wherever he went his heedless ignorance, and the gross misconduct of his followers, left behind implacable hostility, and turned all friendship into bitterness. At last he entered Naples, and seemed to have asserted to the full the French claim to be supreme in Italy, whereas at that very time his position had become completely untenable. A league of Italian States was formed behind his back; Lodovico il Moro, Ferdinand of Naples, the Emperor, Pope Alexander VI., Ferdinand and Isabella, who were now welding Spain into a great and united monarchy, all combined against France; and in presence of this formidable confederacy Charles VIII. had to cut his way home as promptly as he could. At Fornovo, north of the Apennines, he defeated the allies in July, 1495; and by November the main French army had got safely out of Italy. The forces left behind in Naples were worn out by war and pestilence, and the poor remnant of these, too, bringing with them the seeds of horrible contagious diseases, forced their way back to France in 1496. It was the last effort of the King. His health was ruined by debauchery in Italy, repeated in France; and yet, towards the end of his reign, he not merely introduced Italian arts, but attempted to reform the State, to rule prudently, to solace the poor; wherefore, when he died in 1498, the people lamented him greatly, for he had been kindly and affable, brave also on the battle-field; and much is forgiven to a king.

His children died before him, so that Louis d'Orleans, his cousin, was nearest heir to the throne, and succeeded as Louis XII. By his accession in 1498 he reunited the fief of Orleans County to the Crown; by marrying Anne of Brittany, his predecessor's widow, he secured also the great duchy of Brittany. The dispensation of Pope Alexander VI., which enabled him to put away his wife Jeanne, second daughter of Louis XI., was brought into France by Caesar Borgia, who gained thereby his title of Duke of Valentinois, a large sum of money, a French bride, and promises of support in his great schemes in Italy.

His ministers were men of real ability. Georges d'Amboise, Archbishop of Rouen, the chief of them, was a prudent and a sagacious ruler, who, however, unfortunately wanted to be Pope, and urged the King in the direction of Italian politics, which he would have done much better to have left alone. Louis XII. was lazy and of small intelligence; Georges d'Amboise and Caesar Borgia, with their Italian ambitions, easily made him take up a spirited foreign policy which was disastrous at home.

Utterly as the last Italian expedition had failed, the French people were not yet weary of the adventure, and preparations for a new war began at once. In 1499 the King crossed the Alps into the Milanese, and carried all before him for a while. The duchy at first accepted him with enthusiasm; but in 1500 it had had enough of the French and recalled Lodovico, who returned in triumph to Milan. The Swiss mercenaries, however, betrayed him at Novara into the hands of Louis XII., who carried him off to France. The triumph of the French in 1500 was also the highest point of the fortunes of their ally, Caesar Borgia, who seemed for a while to be completely successful. In this year Louis made a treaty at Granada, by which he and Ferdinand the Catholic agreed to despoil Frederick of Naples; and in 1501 Louis made a second expedition into Italy. Again all seemed easy at the outset, and he seized the kingdom of Naples without difficulty; falling out, however, with his partner in the bad bargain, Ferdinand the Catholic, he was speedily swept completely out of the peninsula, with terrible loss of honour, men, and wealth.

It now became necessary to arrange for the future of France. Louis XII. had only a daughter, Claude, and it was proposed that she should be affianced to Charles of Austria, the future statesman and emperor. This scheme formed the basis of the three treaties of Blois (1504). In 1500, by the Treaty of Granada, Louis had in fact handed Naples over to Spain; now by the three treaties he alienated his best friends, the Venetians and the papacy, while he in fact also handed Milan over to the Austrian House, together with territories considered to be integral parts of France. The marriage with Charles came to nothing; the good sense of some, the popular feeling in the country, the open expressions of the States General of Tours, in 1506, worked against the marriage, which had no strong advocate except Queen Anne. Claude, on intercession of the Estates, was affianced to Frangois d'Angouleme, her distant cousin, the heir presumptive to the throne.

In 1507 Louis made war on Venice; and in the following year the famous Treaty of Cambrai was signed by Georges d'Amboise and Margaret of Austria. It was an agreement for a partition of the Venetian territories,—one of the most shameless public deeds in history. The Pope, the King of Aragon, Maximilian, Louis XII., were each to have a share. The war was pushed on with great vigour: the battle of Agnadello (14th May, 1509) cleared the King's way towards Venice; Louis was received with open arms by the North Italian towns, and pushed forward to within eight of Venice. The other Princes came up on every side; the proud "Queen of the Adriatic" was compelled to shrink within her walls, and wait till time dissolved the league. This was not long. The Pope, Julius II., had no wish to hand Northern Italy over to France; he had joined in the shameless league of Cambrai because he wanted to wrest the Romagna cities from Venice, and because he hoped to entirely destroy the ancient friendship between Venice and France. Successful in both aims, he now withdrew from the league, made peace with the Venetians, and stood forward as the head of a new Italian combination, with the Swiss for his fighting men. The strife was close and hot between Pope and King; Louis XII. lost his chief adviser and friend, Georges d'Amboise, the splendid churchman of the age, the French Wolsey; he thought no weapon better than the dangerous one of a council, with claims opposed to those of the papacy; first a National Council at Tours, then an attempted General Council at Pisa, were called on to resist the papal claims. In reply Julius II. created the Holy League of 1511, with Ferdinand of Aragon, Henry VIII. of England, and the Venetians as its chief members, against the French. Louis XII. showed vigour; he sent his nephew Gaston de Foix to subdue the Romagna and threaten the Venetian territories. At the battle of Ravenna, in 1512, Gaston won a brilliant victory and lost his life. From that moment disaster dogged the footsteps of the French in Italy, and before winter they had been driven completely out of the peninsula; the succession of the Medicean Pope, Leo X., to Julius II., seemed to promise the continuance of a policy hostile to France in Italy. Another attempt on Northern Italy proved but another failure, although now Louis XII., taught by his mishaps, had secured the alliance of Venice; the disastrous defeat of La Tremoille, near Novara (1513), compelled the French once more to withdraw beyond the Alps. In this same year an army under the Duc de Longueville, endeavouring to relieve Therouenne, besieged by the English and Maximilian, the Emperor-elect, was caught and crushed at Guinegate. A diversion in favour of Louis XII., made by James IV. of Scotland, failed completely; the Scottish King was defeated and slain at Flodden Field. While his northern frontier was thus exposed, Louis found equal danger threatening him on the east; on this aide, however, he managed to buy off the Swiss, who had attacked the duchy of Burgundy. He was also reconciled with the papacy and the House of Austria. Early in 1514 the death of Anne of Brittany, his spouse, a lady of high ambitions, strong artistic tastes, and humane feelings towards her Bretons, but a bad Queen for France, cleared the way for changes. Claude, the King's eldest daughter, was now definitely married to Francois d'Angouleme, and invested with the duchy of Brittany; and the King himself, still hoping for a male heir to succeed him, married again, wedding Mary

Tudor, the lovely young sister of Henry VIII. This marriage was probably the chief cause of his death, which followed on New Year's day, 1515. His was, in foreign policy, an inglorious and disastrous reign; at home, a time of comfort and material prosperity. Agriculture flourished, the arts of Italy came in, though (save in architecture) France could claim little artistic glory of her own; the organisation of justice and administration was carried out; in letters and learning France still lagged behind her neighbours.

The heir to the crown was Francois d'Angouleme, great-grandson of that Louis d'Orleans who had been assassinated in the bad days of the strife between Burgundians and Armagnacs, in 1407, and great-great-grandson of Charles V. of France. He was still young, very eager to be king, very full of far-reaching schemes. Few things in history are more striking than the sudden change, at this moment, from the rule of middle- aged men or (as men of fifty were then often called) old men, to the rule of youths,—from sagacious, worldly-prudent monarchs—to impulsive boys, —from Henry VII. to Henry VIII., from Louis XII. to Frangois I, from Ferdinand to Charles.

On the whole, Frangois I. was the least worthy of the three. He was brilliant, "the king of culture," apt scholar in Renaissance art and immorality; brave, also, and chivalrous, so long as the chivalry involved no self-denial, for he was also thoroughly selfish, and his personal aims and ideas were mean. His reign was to be a reaction from that of Louis XII.

From the beginning, Francois chose his chief officers unwisely. In Antoine du Prat, his new chancellor, he had a violent and lawless adviser; in Charles de Bourbon, his new constable, an untrustworthy commander. Forthwith he plunged into Italian politics, being determined to make good his claim both to Naples and to Milan; he made most friendly arrangements with the Archduke Charles, his future rival, promising to help him in securing, when the time came, the vast inheritances of his two grandfathers, Maximilian, the Emperor-elect, and Ferdinand of Aragon; never was a less wise agreement entered upon. This done, the Italian war began; Francois descended into Italy, and won the brilliant battle of Marignano, in which the French chivalry crushed the Swiss burghers and peasant mercenaries. The French then overran the north of Italy, and, in conjunction with the Venetians, carried all before them. But the triumphs of the sword were speedily wrested from him by the adroitness of the politician; in an interview with Leo X. at Bologna, Francois bartered the liberties of the Gallican Church for shadowy advantages in Italy. The 'Pragmatic Sanction of Bourgea', which now for nearly a century had secured to the Church of France independence in the choice of her chief officers, was replaced by a concordat, whereby the King allowed the papacy once more to drain the wealth of the Church of France, while the Pope allowed the King almost autocratic power over it. He was to appoint to all benefices, with exception of a few privileged offices; the Pope was no longer to be threatened with general councils, while he should receive again the annates of the Church.

The years which followed this brilliantly disastrous opening brought little good to France. In 1516 the death of Ferdinand the Catholic placed Charles on the throne of Spain; in 1519 the death of Maximilian threw open to the young Princes the most dazzling prize of human ambition,—the headship of the Holy Roman Empire. Francois I., Charles, and Henry VIII. were all candidates for the votes of the seven electors, though the last never seriously entered the lists. The struggle lay between Francois, the brilliant young Prince, who seemed to represent the new opinions in literature and art, and Charles of Austria and Spain, who was as yet unknown and despised, and, from his education under the virtuous and scholastic Adrian of Utrecht, was thought likely to represent the older and reactionary opinions of the clergy. After a long and sharp competition, the great prize fell to Charles, henceforth known to history as that great monarch and emperor, Charles V.

The rivalry between the Princes could not cease there. Charles, as representative of the House of Burgundy, claimed all that had been lost when Charles the Bold fell; and in 1521 the war broke out between him and Francois, the first of a series of struggles between the two rivals. While the King wasted the resources of his country on these wars, his proud and unwise mother, Louise of Savoy, guided by Antoine du Prat, ruled, to the sorrow of all, at home. The war brought no glory with it: on the Flemish frontier a place or two was taken; in Biscay Fontarabia fell before the arms of France; in Italy Francois had to meet a new league of Pope and Emperor, and his troops were swept completely out of the Milanese. In the midst of all came the defection of that great prince, the Constable de Bourbon, head of the younger branch of the Bourbon House, the most powerful feudal lord in France. Louise of Savoy had enraged and offended him, or he her; the King slighted him, and in 1523 the Constable made a secret treaty with Charles V. and Henry VIII., and, taking flight into Italy, joined the Spaniards under Lannoy. The French, who had again invaded the Milanese, were again driven out in 1524; on the other hand, the incursions of the imperialists into Picardy, Provence, and the southeast were all complete failures. Encouraged by the repulse of Bourbon from Marseilles, Francois I. once more crossed the Alps, and overran a great part of the valley of the Po; at the siege of Pavia he was attacked by Pescara and Bourbon, utterly defeated and taken prisoner (24th February, 1525); the broken remnants of the French were swept out of Italy at once, and Francois I. was carried into

Spain, a captive at Madrid. His mother, best in adversity, behaved with high pride and spirit; she overawed disaffection, made preparations for resistance, looked out for friends on every side. Had Francois been in truth a hero, he might, even as a prisoner, have held his own; but he was unable to bear the monotony of confinement, and longed for the pleasures of France. On this mean nature Charles V. easily worked, and made the captive monarch sign the Treaty of Madrid (January 14, 1526), a compact which Francois meant to break as soon as he could, for he knew neither heroism nor good faith. The treaty stipulated that Francois should give up the duchy of Burgundy to Charles, and marry Eleanor of Portugal, Charles's sister; that Francois should also abandon his claims on Flanders, Milan, and Naples, and should place two sons in the Emperor's hands as hostages. Following the precedent of Louis XI. in the case of Normandy, he summoned an assembly of nobles and the Parliament of Paris to Cognac, where they declared the cession of Burgundy to be impossible. He refused to return to Spain, and made alliances wherever he could, with the Pope, with Venice, Milan, and England. The next year saw the ruin of this league in the discomfiture of Clement VII., and the sack of Rome by the German mercenaries under Bourbon, who was killed in the assault. The war went on till 1529, when Francois, having lost two armies in it, and gained nothing but loss and harm, was willing for peace; Charles V., alarmed at the progress of the Turks, was not less willing; and in August, 1529, the famous Treaty, of Cambrai, "the Ladies' Peace," was agreed to by Margaret of Austria and Louise of Savoy. Though Charles V. gave up all claim on the duchy of Burgundy, he had secured to himself Flanders and Artois, and had entirely cleared French influences out of Italy, which now became firmly fixed under the imperial hand, as a connecting link between his Spanish and German possessions. Francois lost ground and credit by these successive treaties, conceived in bad faith, and not honestly carried out.

No sooner had the Treaty of Cambrai been effectual in bringing his sons back to France, than Francois began to look out for new pretexts and means for war. Affairs were not unpromising. His mother's death in 1531 left him in possession of a huge fortune, which she had wrung from defenceless France; the powers which were jealous of Austria, the Turk, the English King, the members of the Smalkald league, all looked to Francois as their leader; Clement VII., though his misfortunes had thrown him into the Emperor's hands, was not unwilling to treat with France; and in 1533 by the compact of Marseilles the Pope broke up the friendship between Francois and Henry VIII., while he married his niece Catherine de' Medici to Henri, the second son of Francois. This compact was a real disaster to France; the promised dowry of Catherine—certain Italian cities—was never paid, and the death of Clement VII. in 1534 made the political alliance with the papacy a failure. The influence of Catherine affected and corrupted

French history for half a century. Preparations for war went on; Francois made a new scheme for a national army, though in practice he preferred the tyrant's arm, the foreign mercenary. From his day till the Revolution the French army was largely composed of bodies of men tempted out of other countries, chiefly from Switzerland or Germany.

While the Emperor strove to appease the Protestant Princes of Germany by the Peace of Kadan (1534), Francois strengthened himself with a definite alliance with Soliman; and when, on the death of Francesco Sforza, Duke of Milan, who left no heirs, Charles seized the duchy as its overlord, Francois, after some boot-less negotiation, declared war on his great rival (1536). His usual fortunes pre-vailed so long as he was the attacking party: his forces were soon swept out of Piedmont, and the Emperor carried the war over the frontier into Provence. That also failed, and Charles was fain to withdraw after great losses into Italy. The defence of Provence—a defence which took the form of a ruthless destruction of all its resources—had been entrusted to Anne de Montmorency, who hencefor-ward became Constable of France, and exerted great influence over Francois I. Though these two campaigns, the French in Italy and the imperialist in Provence, had equally failed in 1536, peace did not follow till 1538, when, after the terrible defeat of Ferdinand of Austria by the Turks, Charles was anxious to have free hand in Germany. Under the mediation of Paul III. the agreement of Nice was come to, which included a ten years' truce and the abandonment by Francois of all his foreign allies and aims. He seemed a while to have fallen completely under the influence of the sagacious Emperor. He gave way entirely to the Church party of the time, a party headed by gloomy Henri, now Dauphin, who never lost the impress of his Spanish captivity, and by the Constable Anne de Montmorency; for a time the artistic or Renaissance party, represented by Anne, Duchesse d'Etampes, and Catherine de' Medici, fell into disfavour. The Emperor even ven-tured to pass through France, on his way from Spain to the Netherlands. All this friendship, however, fell to dust, when it was found that Charles refused to invest the Duc d'Orleans, the second son of Francois, with the duchy of Milan, and when the Emperor's second expedition against the sea-power of the Turks had proved a complete failure, and Charles had returned to Spain with loss of all his fleet and army. Then Francois hesitated no longer, and declared war against him (1541). The shock the Emperor had suffered inspirited all his foes; the Sultan and the Protestant German Princes were all eager for war; the influence of Anne de Montmorency had to give way before that of the House of Guise, that frontier family, half French, half German, which was destined to play a large part in the troubled history of the coming half-century. Claude, Duc de Guise, a veteran of the earliest days of Francois, was vehemently opposed to Charles and the Austro-Spanish power, and ruled in the King's councils. This last war was as mischievous

as its predecessors no great battles were fought; in the frontier affairs the combat-
ants were about equally fortunate; the battle of Cerisolles, won by the French
under Enghien (1544), was the only considerable success they had, and even that
was almost barren of results, for the danger to Northern France was imminent;
there a combined invasion had been planned and partly executed by Charles and
Henry VIII., and the country, almost undefended, was at their mercy. The two
monarchs, however, distrusted one another; and Charles V., anxious about
Germany, sent to Francois proposals for peace from Crespy Couvrant, near Laon,
where he had halted his army; Francois, almost in despair, gladly made terms with
him. The King gave up his claims on Flanders and Artois, the Emperor his on the
duchy of Burgundy; the King abandoned his old Neapolitan ambition, and
Charles promised one of the Princesses of the House of Austria, with Milan as her
dower, to the Duc d'Orleans, second son of Francois. The Duke dying next year,
this portion of the agreement was not carried out. The Peace of Crespy, which
ended the wars between the two great rivals, was signed in autumn, 1544, and,
like the wars which led to it, was indecisive and lame.

Charles learnt that with all his great power he could not strike a fatal blow at
France; France ought to have learnt that she was very weak for foreign conquest,
and that her true business was to consolidate and develop her power at home.
Henry VIII. deemed himself wronged by this independent action on the part of
Charles, who also had his grievances with the English monarch; he stood out till
1546, and then made peace with Francois, with the aim of forming a fresh combination against Charles. In the midst of new projects and much activity, the mar-
rer of man's plots came on the scene, and carried off in the same year, 1547, the
English King and Francois I., leaving Charles V. undisputed arbiter of the affairs
of Europe. In this same year he also crushed the Protestant Princes at the battle of
Muhlberg.

In the reign of Francois I. the Court looked not unkindly on the Reformers, more
particularly in the earlier years.

Henri II., who succeeded in 1547, "had all the faults of his father, with a weaker
mind;" and as strength of mind was not one of the characteristics of Francois I.,
we may imagine how little firmness there was in the gloomy King who now
reigned. Party spirit ruled at Court. Henri II., with his ancient mistress, Diane de
Poitiers, were at the head of one party, that of the strict Catholics, and were supported by old Anne de Montmorency, most unlucky of soldiers, most fanatical of
Catholics, and by the Guises, who chafed a good deal under the stern rule of the
Constable. This party had almost extinguished its antagonists; in the struggle of
the mistresses, the pious and learned Anne d'Etampes had to give place to impe-

rious Diane, Catherine, the Queen, was content to bide her time, watching with Italian coolness the game as it went on; of no account beside her rival, and yet quite sure to have her day, and ready to play parties against one another. Meanwhile, she brought to her royal husband ten sickly children, most of whom died young, and three wore the crown. Of the many bad things she did for France, that was perhaps among the worst.

On the accession of Henri II. the duchy of Brittany finally lost even nominal independence; he next got the hand of Mary, Queen of Scots, then but five years old, for the Dauphin Francois; she was carried over to France; and being by birth half a Guise, by education and interests of her married life she became entirely French. It was a great triumph for Henri, for the Protector Somerset had laid his plans to secure her for young Edward VI.; it was even more a triumph for the Guises, who saw opened out a broad and clear field for their ambition.

At first Henri II. showed no desire for war, and seemed to shrink from rivalry or collision with Charles V. He would not listen to Paul III., who, in his anxiety after the fall of the Protestant power in Germany in 1547, urged him to resist the Emperor's triumphant advance; he seemed to show a dread of war, even among his neighbours. After he had won his advantage over Edward VI., he escaped the war which seemed almost inevitable, recovered Boulogne from the English by a money payment, and smoothed the way for peace between England and Scotland. He took much interest in the religious question, and treated the Calvinists with great severity; he was also occupied by troubles in the south and west of France. Meanwhile, a new Pope, Julius III., was the weak dependent of the Emperor, and there seemed to be no head left for any movement against the universal domination of Charles V. His career from 1547 to 1552 was, to all appearance, a triumphal march of unbroken success. Yet Germany was far from acquiescence; the Princes were still discontented and watchful; even Ferdinand of Austria, his brother, was offended by the Emperor's anxiety to secure everything, even the imperial crown for his son Philip; Maurice of Saxony, that great problem of the age, was preparing for a second treachery, or, it may be, for a patriotic effort. These German malcontents now appealed to Henri for aid; and at last Henri seemed inclined to come. He had lately made alliance with England, and in 1552 formed a league at Chambord with the German Princes; the old connection with the Turk was also talked of. The Germans agreed to allow' him to hold (as imperial vicar, not as King of France) the "three bishoprics," Metz, Verdun, and Toul; he also assumed a protectorate over the spiritual princes, those great bishops and electors of the Rhine, whose stake in the Empire was so important. The general lines of French foreign politics are all here clearly marked; in this Henri II. is the forerunner of Henri IV. and of Louis XIV.; the imperial politics of Napoleon start from much the same lines; the proclamations of Napoleon III. before the Franco-German war seemed like thin echoes of the same.

Early in 1552 Maurice of Saxony struck his great blow at his master in the Tyrol, destroying in an instant all the Emperor's plans for the suppression of Lutheran opinions, and the reunion of Germany in a Catholic empire; and while Charles V. fled for his life, Henri II. with a splendid army crossed the frontiers of Lorraine. Anne de Montmorency, whose opposition to the war had been overborne by the Guises, who warmly desired to see a French predominance in Lorraine, was sent forward to reduce Metz, and quickly got that important city into his hands; Toul and Verdun soon opened their gates, and were secured in reality, if not in name, to France. Eager to undertake a protectorate of the Rhine, Henri II. tried also to lay hands on Strasburg; the citizens, however, resisted, and he had to withdraw; the same fate befell his troops in an attempt on Spires. Still, Metz and the line of the Vosges mountains formed a splendid acquisition for France. The French army, leaving strong garrisons in Lorraine, withdrew through Luxemburg and the northern frontier; its remaining exploits were few and mean, for the one gleam of good fortune enjoyed by Anne de Montmorency, who was unwise and arrogant, and a most inefficient commander, soon deserted him. Charles V., as soon as he could gather forces, laid siege to Metz, but, after nearly three months of late autumnal operations, was fain to break up and withdraw, baffled and with loss of half his army, across the Rhine. Though some success attended his arms on the northern frontier, it was of no permanent value; the loss of Metz, and the failure in the attempt to take it, proved to the worn-out Emperor that the day of his power and opportunity was past. The conclusions of the Diet of Augsburg in 1555 settled for half a century the struggle between Lutheran and Catholic, but settled it in a way not at all to his mind; for it was the safeguard of princely interests against his plans for an imperial unity. Weary of the losing strife, yearning for ease, ordered by his physicians to withdraw from active life, Charles in the course of 1555 and 1556 resigned all his great lordships and titles, leaving Philip his son to succeed him in Italy, the Netherlands, and Spain, and his brother Ferdinand of Austria to wear in his stead the imperial diadem. These great changes sundered awhile the interests of Austria from those of Spain.

Henri endeavoured to take advantage of the check in the fortunes of his antagonists; he sent Anne de Montmorency to support Gaspard de Coligny, the Admiral of France, in Picardy, and in harmony with Paul IV., instructed Francois, Duc de Guise, to enter Italy to oppose the Duke of Alva. As of old, the French arms at first carried all before them, and Guise, deeming himself heir to the crown of Naples (for he was the eldest great-grandson of Rene II., titular King of Naples), pushed eagerly forward as far as the Abruzzi. There he was met and outgeneraled by Alva, who drove him back to Rome, whence he was now recalled by urgent summons to France; for the great disaster of St. Quentin had laid Paris itself open to the assault of an enterprising enemy. With the departure of Guise from Italy the age of the Italian expeditions comes to an end. On the northern side of the realm things had gone just as badly. Philibert of Savoy, commanding for Philip with Spanish and English troops, marched into France as far as to the Somme, and laid siege to St. Quentin, which was bravely defended by Amiral de Coligny. Anne de Montmorency, coming up to relieve the place, managed his movements so clumsily that he was caught by Count Egmont and the Flemish horse, and, with incredibly small loss to the conquerors, was utterly routed (1557). Montmorency himself and a crowd of nobles and soldiers were taken; the slaughter was great. Coligny made a gallant and tenacious stand in the town itself, but at last was overwhelmed, and the place fell. Terrible as these mishaps were to France, Philip II. was not of a temper to push an advantage vigorously; and while his army lingered, Francois de Guise came swiftly back from Italy; and instead of wasting strength in a doubtful attack on the allies in Picardy, by a sudden stroke of genius he assaulted and took Calais (January, 1558), and swept the English finally off the soil of France. This unexpected and brilliant blow cheered and solaced the afflicted country, while it finally secured the ascendency of the House of Guise. The Duke's brother, the Cardinal de Lorraine, carried all before him in the King's councils; the Dauphin, betrothed long before, was now married to Mary of Scots; a secret treaty bound the young Queen to bring her kingdom over with her; it was thought that France with Scotland would be at least a match for England joined with Spain. In the same year, 1558, the French advance along the coast, after they had taken Dunkirk and Nieuport, was finally checked by the brilliant genius of Count Egmont, who defeated them at Gravelinea. All now began to wish for peace, especially Montmorency, weary of being a prisoner, and anxious to get back to Court, that he might check the fortunes of the Guises; Philip desired it that he might have free hand against heresy. And so, at Cateau-Cambresis, a peace was made in April, 1559, by which France retained the three bishoprics and Calais, surrendering Thionville, Montmedy, and one or two other frontier towns, while she recovered Ham and St. Quentin; the House of Savoy was reinstated by Philip, as a reward to Philibert for his services, and formed a solid barrier for a time between France and Italy; cross-marriages between Spain, France, and Savoy were arranged;—and finally, the treaty contained secret articles by which the Guises for France and Granvella for the Netherlands agreed to crush heresy with a strong hand. As a sequel to this peace, Henri II. held a great tournament at Paris, at which he was accidentally slain by a Scottish knight in the lists.

The Guises now shot up into abounded power. On the Guise side the Cardinal de Lorraine was the cleverest man, the true head, while Francois, the Duke, was the arm; he showed leanings towards the Lutherans. On the other side, the head was the dull and obstinate Anne de Montmorency, the Constable, an unwavering Catholic, supported by the three Coligny brothers, who all were or became Huguenots. The Queen- mother Catherine fluctuated uneasily between the parties, and though Catholic herself, or rather not a Protestant, did not hesitate to befriend the Huguenots, if the political arena seemed to need their gallant swords. Their noblest leader was Coligny, the admiral; their recognised head was Antoine, King of Navarre, a man as foolish as fearless. He was heir presumptive to the throne after the Valois boys, and claimed to have charge of the young King. Though the Guises had the lead at first, the Huguenots seemed, from their strong aristocratic connections, to have the fairer prospects before them.

Thirty years of desolate civil strife are before us, and we must set it all down briefly and drily. The prelude to the troubles was played by the Huguenots, who in 1560, guided by La Renaudie, a Perigord gentleman, formed a plot to carry off the young King; for Francois II. had already treated them with considerable severity, and had dismissed from his councils both the princes of the blood royal and the Constable de Montmorency. The plot failed miserably and La Renaudie lost his life; it only secured more firmly the authority of the Guises. As a counterpoise to their influence, the Queen-mother now conferred the vacant chancellorship on one of the wisest men France has ever seen, her Lord Bacon, Michel de L'Hopital, a man of the utmost prudence and moderation, who, had the times been better, might have won constitutional liberties for his country, and appeased her civil strife. As it was, he saved her from the Inquisition; his hand drew the edicts which aimed at enforcing toleration on France; he guided the assembly of notables which gathered at Fontainebleau, and induced them to attempt a compromise which moderate Catholics and Calvinists might accept, and which might lessen the power of the Guises. This assembly was followed by a meeting of the States General at Orleans, at which the Prince de Conde and the King of Navarre were seized by the Guises on a charge of having had to do with La Renaudie's plot. It would have gone hard with them had not the sickly King at this very time fallen ill and died (1560).

This was a grievous blow to the Guises. Now, as in a moment, all was shattered; Catherine de Medici rose at once to the command of affairs; the new King, Charles IX., was only, ten years old, and her position as Regent was assured. The Guises would gladly have ruled with her, but she had no fancy for that; she and Chancellor de L'Hopital were not likely to ally themselves with all that was severe and repressive. It must not be forgotten that the best part of her policy was inspired by the Chancellor de L'Hopital.

Now it was that Mary Stuart, the Queen-dowager, was compelled to leave France for Scotland; her departure clearly marks the fall of the Guises; and it also showed Philip of Spain that it was no longer necessary for him to refuse aid and counsel to the Guises; their claims were no longer formidable to him on the larger sphere of European politics; no longer could Mary Stuart dream of wearing the triple crown of Scotland, France, and England.

The tolerant language of L'Hopital at the States General of Orleans in 1561 satisfied neither side. The Huguenots were restless; the Bourbon Princes tried to crush the Guises, in return for their own imprisonment the year before; the Constable was offended by the encouragement shown to the Huguenots; it was plain that new changes impended. Montmorency began them by going over to the Guises; and the fatal triumvirate of Francois, Duc de Guise, Montmorency, and St. Andre the marshal, was formed. We find the King of Spain forthwith entering the field of French intrigues and politics, as the support and stay of this triumvirate. Parties take a simpler format once, one party of Catholics and another of Huguenots, with the Queen-mother and the moderates left powerless between them. These last, guided still by L'Hopital, once more convoked the States General at Pontoise: the nobles and the Third Estate seemed to side completely with the Queen and the moderates; a controversy between Huguenots and Jesuits at Poissy only added to the discontent of the Catholics, who were now joined by foolish Antoine, King of Navarre. The edict of January, 1562, is the most remarkable of the attempts made by the Queen-mother to satisfy the Huguenots; but party-passion was already too strong for it to succeed; civil war had become inevitable.

The period may be divided into four parts: (1) the wars before the establishment of the League (1562-1570); (2) the period of the St. Bartholomew (1570-1573); (3) the struggle of the new Politique party against the Leaguers (1573-1559); (4) the efforts of Henri IV. to crush the League and reduce the country to peace (1589-1595). The period can also be divided by that series of agreements, or peaces, which break it up into eight wars:

1. The war of 1562, on the skirts of which Philip of Spain interfered on one side, and Queen Elizabeth with the Calvinistic German Princes on the other, showed at once that the Huguenots were by far the weaker party. The English troops at Havre enabled them at first to command the lower Seine up to Rouen; but the other party, after a long siege which cost poor Antoine of Navarre his life, took that place, and relieved Paris of anxiety. The Huguenots had also spread far and wide over the south and west, occupying Orleans; the bridge of Orleans was their point of junction between Poitou and Germany. While the strength of the

Catholics lay to the east, in Picardy, and at Paris, the Huguenot power was mostly concentrated in the south and west of France. Conde, who commanded at
Orleans, supported by German allies, made an attempt on Paris, but finding the
capital too strong for him, turned to the west, intending to join the English troops
from Havre. Montmorency, however, caught him at Dreux; and in the battle that
ensued, the Marshal of France, Saint-Andre, perished; Conde was captured by the
Catholics, Montmorency by the Huguenots. Coligny, the admiral, drew off his
defeated troops with great skill, and fell back to beyond the Loire; the Duc de
Guise remained as sole head of the Catholics. Pushing on his advantage, the Duke
immediately laid siege to Orleans, and there he fell by the hand of a Huguenot
assassin. Both parties had suffered so much that the Queen- mother thought she
might interpose with terms of peace; the Edict of Amboise (March, 1563) closed
the war, allowing the Calvinists freedom of worship in the towns they held, and
some other scanty privileges. A three years' quiet followed, though all men suspected their neighbours, and the high Catholic party tried hard to make
Catherine sacrifice L'Hopital and take sharp measures with the Huguenots. They
on their side were restless and suspicious, and it was felt that another war could
not be far off. Intrigues were incessant, all men thinking to make their profit out
of the weakness of France. The struggle between Calvinists and Catholics in the
Netherlands roused much feeling, though Catherine refused to favour either
party. She collected an army of her own; it was rumoured that she intended to
take the Huguenots by surprise and annihilate them. In autumn, 1567, their
patience gave way, and they raised the standard of revolt, in harmony with the
heroic Netherlanders. Conde and the Chatillons beleaguered Paris from the
north, and fought the battle of St. Denis, in which the old Constable, Anne de
Montmorency, was killed. The Huguenots, however, were defeated and forced to
withdraw, Conde marching eastward to join the German troops now coming up
to his aid. No more serious fighting followed; the Peace of Longjumeau (March,
1568), closed the second war, leaving matters much as they were. The aristocratic resistance against the Catholic sovereigns, against what is often called the
"Catholic Reaction," had proved itself hollow; in Germany and the Netherlands,
as well as in France, the Protestant cause seemed to fail; it was not until the religious question became mixed up with questions as to political rights and freedom,
as in the Low Countries, that a new spirit of hope began to spring up.

The Peace of Longjumeau gave no security to the Huguenot nobles; they felt that
the assassin might catch them any day. An attempt to seize Condo and Coligny
failed, and served only to irritate their party; Cardinal Chatillon escaped to
England; Jeanne of Navarre and her young son Henri took refuge at La Rochelle;
L'Hopital was dismissed the Court. The Queen-mother seemed to have thrown
off her cloak of moderation, and to be ready to relieve herself of the Huguenots

by any means, fair or foul. War accordingly could not fail to break out again before the end of the year. Conde had never been so strong; with his friends in England and the Low Countries, and the enthusiastic support of a great party of nobles and religious adherents at home, his hopes rose; he even talked of deposing the Valois and reigning in their stead. He lost his life, however, early in 1569, at the battle of Jarnac. Coligny once more with difficulty, as at Dreux, saved the broken remnants of the defeated Huguenots. Conde's death, regarded at the time by the Huguenots as an irreparable calamity, proved in the end to be no serious loss; for it made room for the true head of the party, Henri of Navarre. No sooner had Jeanne of Navarre heard of the mishap of Jarnac than she came into the Huguenot camp and presented to the soldiers her young son Henri and the young Prince de Conde, a mere child. Her gallant bearing and the true soldier-spirit of Coligny, who shone most brightly in adversity, restored their temper; they even won some small advantages. Before long, however, the Duc d'Anjou, the King's youngest brother, caught and punished them severely at Moncontour. Both parties thenceforward wore themselves out with desultory warfare. In August, 1570, the Peace of St. Germain-en-Laye closed the third war and ended the first period.

2. It was the most favourable Peace the Huguenots had won as yet; it secured them, besides previous rights, four strongholds. The Catholics were dissatisfied; they could not sympathise with the Queen-mother in her alarm at the growing strength of Philip II., head of the Catholics in Europe; they dreaded the existence and growing influence of a party now beginning to receive a definite name, and honourable nickname, the Politiques. These were that large body of French gentlemen who loved the honour of their country rather than their religious party, and who, though Catholics, were yet moderate and tolerant. A pair of marriages now proposed by the Court amazed them still more. It was suggested that the Duc d'Anjou should marry Queen Elizabeth of England, and Henri of Navarre, Marguerite de Valois, the King's sister. Charles II. hoped thus to be rid of his brother, whom he disliked, and to win powerful support against Spain, by the one match, and by the other to bring the civil wars to a close. The sketch of a far-reaching resistance to Philip II. was drawn out; so convinced of his good faith was the prudent and sagacious William of Orange, that, on the strength of these plans, he refused good terms now offered him by Spain. The Duc d'Alencon, the remaining son of Catherine, the brother who did not come to the throne, was deeply interested in the plans for a war in the Netherlands; Anjou, who had withdrawn from the scheme of marriage with Queen Elizabeth, was at this moment a candidate for the throne of Poland; while negotiations respecting it were going on, Marguerite de Valois was married to Henri of Navarre, the worst of wives [?? D.W.] to a husband none too good. Coligny, who had strongly opposed the candidature of Anjou for the throne of Poland, was set on by an assassin, employed

by the Queen-mother and her favourite son, and badly wounded; the Huguenots were in utmost alarm, filling the air with cries and menaces. Charles showed great concern for his friend's recovery, and threatened vengeance on the assassins. What was his astonishment to learn that those assassins were his mother and brother! Catherine worked on his fears, and the plot for the great massacre was combined in an instant. The very next day after the King's consent was wrung from him, 24th August, 1572, the massacre of St. Bartholomew's day took place. The murder of Coligny was completed; his son-in-law Teligny perished; all the chief Huguenots were slain; the slaughter spread to country towns; the Church and the civil power were at one, and the victims, taken at unawares, could make no resistance. The two Bourbons, Henri and the Prince de Conde, were spared; they bought their lives by a sudden conversion to Catholicism. The chief guilt of this great crime lies with Catherine de' Medici; for, though it is certain that she did not plan it long before, assassination was a recognised part of her way of dealing with Huguenots.

A short war followed, a revolt of the southern cities rather than a war. They made tenacious and heroic resistance; a large part of the royal forces sympathised rather with them than with the League; and in July, 1573, the Edict of Boulogne granted them even more than they, had been promised by the Peace of St. Germain.

3. We have reached the period of the "Wan of the League," as the four later civil wars are often called. The last of the four is alone of any real importance.

Just as the Peace of La Rochelle was concluded, the Duc d'Anjou, having been elected King of Poland, left France; it was not long before troubles began again. The Duc d'Alencon was vexed by his mother's neglect; as heir presumptive to the crown he thought he deserved better treatment, and sought to give himself consideration by drawing towards the middle party; Catherine seemed to be intriguing for the ruin of that party— nothing was safe while she was moving. The King had never held up his head since the St. Bartholomew; it was seen that he now was dying, and the Queen-mother took the opportunity of laying hands on the middle party. She arrested Alencon, Montmorency, and Henri of Navarre, together with some lesser chiefs; in the midst of it all Charles IX. died (1574), in misery, leaving the ill-omened crown to Henri of Anjou, King of Poland, his next brother, his mother's favourite, the worst of a bad breed. At the same time the fifth civil war broke out, interesting chiefly because it was during its continuance that the famous League was actually formed.

Henri III., when he heard of his brother's death, was only too eager to slip away like a culprit from Poland, though he showed no alacrity in returning to France, and dallied with the pleasures of Italy for months. An attempt to draw him over to the side of the Politiques failed completely; he attached himself on the contrary to the Guises, and plunged into the grossest dissipation, while he posed himself before men as a good and zealous Catholic. The Politiques and Huguenots therefore made a compact in 1575, at Milhaud on the Tarn, and chose the Prince de Conde as their head; Henri of Navarre escaped from Paris, threw off his forced Catholicism, and joined them. Against them the strict Catholics seemed powerless; the Queen-mother closed this war with the Peace of Chastenoy (May, 1576), with terms unusually favourable for both Politiques and Huguenots: for the latter, free worship throughout France, except at Paris; for the chiefs of the former, great governments, for Alencon a large central district, for Conde, Picardy, for Henri of Navarre, Guienne.

To resist all this the high Catholic party framed the League they had long been meditating; it is said that the Cardinal de Lorraine had sketched it years before, at the time of the later sittings of the Council of Trent. Lesser compacts had already been made from time to time; now it was proposed to form one great League, towards which all should gravitate. The head of the League was Henri, Duc de Guise the second, "Balafre," who had won that title in fighting against the German reiters the year before, when they entered France under Condo. He certainly hoped at this time to succeed to the throne of France, either by deposing the corrupt and feeble Henri III., "as Pippin dealt with Hilderik," or by seizing the throne, when the King's debaucheries should have brought him to the grave. The Catholics of the more advanced type, and specially the Jesuits, now in the first flush of credit and success, supported him warmly. The headquarters of the movement were in Picardy; its first object, opposition to the establishment of Conde as governor of that province. The League was also very popular with the common folk, especially in the towns of the north. It soon found that Paris was its natural centre; thence it spread swiftly across the whole natural France; it was warmly supported by Philip of Spain. The States General, convoked at Blois in 1576, could bring no rest to France; opinion was just as much divided there as in the country; and the year 1577 saw another petty war, counted as the sixth, which was closed by the Peace of Bergerac, another ineffectual truce which settled nothing. It was a peace made with the Politiques and Huguenots by the Court; it is significant of the new state of affairs that the League openly refused to be bound by it, and continued a harassing, objectless warfare. The Duc d'Anjou (he had taken that title on his brother Henri's accession to the throne) in 1578 deserted the Court party, towards which his mother had drawn him, and made friends with the Calvinists in the Netherlands. The southern provinces named him "Defender of their liberties;" they had hopes he might wed Elizabeth of England; they quite mistook their man. In 1579 "the Gallants' War" broke out; the

Leaguers had it all their own way; but Henri III., not too friendly to them, and urged by his brother Anjou, to whom had been offered sovereignty over the seven united provinces in 1580, offered the insurgents easy terms, and the Treaty of Fleix closed the seventh war. Anjou in the Netherlands could but show his weakness; nothing went well with him; and at last, having utterly wearied out his friends, he fled, after the failure of his attempt to secure Antwerp, into France. There he fell ill of consumption and died in 1584.

This changed at once the complexion of the succession question. Hitherto, though no children seemed likely to be born to him, Henri III. was young and might live long, and his brother was there as his heir. Now, Henri III. was the last Prince of the Valois, and Henri of Navarre in hereditary succession was heir presumptive to the throne, unless the Salic law were to be set aside. The fourth son of Saint Louis, Robert, Comte de Clermont, who married Beatrix, heiress of Bourbon, was the founder of the House of Bourbon. Of this family the two elder branches had died out: John, who had been a central figure in the War of the Public Weal, in 1488; Peter, husband of Anne of France, in 1503; neither of them leaving heirs male. Of the younger branch Francois died in 1525, and the famous Constable de Bourbon in 1527. This left as the only representatives of the family, the Comtes de La Marche; of these the elder had died out in 1438, and the junior alone survived in the Comtes de Vendome. The head of this branch, Charles, was made Duc de Vendome by Francois I. in 1515; he was father of Antoine, Duc de Vendome, who, by marrying the heroic Jeanne d'Albret, became King of Navarre, and of Louis, who founded the House of Conde; lastly, Antoine was the father of Henri IV. He was, therefore, a very distant cousin to Henri III; the Houses of Capet, of Alencon, of Orleans, of Angouleme, of Maine, and of Burgundy, as well as the elder Bourbons, had to fall extinct before Henri of Navarre could become heir to the crown. All this, however, had now happened; and the Huguenots greatly rejoiced in the prospect of a Calvinist King. The Politique party showed no ill-will towards him; both they and the Court party declared that if he would become once more a Catholic they would rally to him; the Guises and the League were naturally all the more firmly set against him; and Henri of Navarre saw that he could not as yet safely endanger his influence with the Huguenots, while his conversion would not disarm the hostility of the League. They had before, this put forward as heir to the throne Henri's uncle, the wretched old Cardinal de Bourbon, who had all the faults and none of the good qualities of his brother Antoine. Under cover of his name the Duc de Guise hoped to secure the succession for himself; he also sold himself and his party to Philip of Spain, who was now in fullest expectation of a final triumph over his foes. He had assassinated William the Silent; any day Elizabeth or Henri of Navarre might be found murdered; the domination of Spain over Europe seemed almost secured.

The pact of Joinville, signed between Philip, Guise, and Mayenne, gives us the measure of the aims of the high Catholic party. Paris warmly sided with them; the new development of the League, the "Sixteen of Paris," one representative for each of the districts of the capital, formed a vigorous organisation and called for the King's deposition; they invited Henri, Duc de Guise, to Paris. Soon after this Henri III. humbled himself, and signed the Treaty of Nemours (1585) with the Leaguers. He hereby became nominal head of the League and its real slave.

The eighth war, the "War of the Three Henries," that is, of Henri III. and Henri de Guise against Henri of Navarre, now broke out. The Pope made his voice heard; Sixtus excommunicated the Bourbons, Henri and Conde, and blessed the Leaguers.

For the first time there was some real life in one of these civil ware, for Henri of Navarre rose nobly to the level of his troubles. At first the balance of successes was somewhat in favour of the Leaguers; the political atmosphere grew even more threatening, and terrible things, like lightning flashes, gleamed out now and again. Such, for example, was the execution of Mary Stuart, Queen of Scots, in 1586. It was known that Philip II. was preparing to crush England. Elizabeth did what she could to support Henri of Navarre; he had the good fortune to win the battle of Contras, in which the Duc de Joyeuse, one of the favourites of Henri III., was defeated and killed. The Duc de Guise, on the other hand, was too strong for the Germans, who had marched into France to join the Huguenots, and defeated them at Vimroy and Auneau, after which he marched in triumph to Paris, in spite of the orders and opposition of. the King, who, finding himself powerless, withdrew to Chartres. Once more Henri III. was obliged to accept such terms as the Leaguers chose to impose; and with rage in his heart he signed the "Edict of Union" (1588), in which he named the Duc de Guise lieutenant-general of the kingdom, and declared that no heretic could succeed to the throne. Unable to endure the humiliation, Henri III. that same winter, assassinated the Duc and the Cardinal de Guise, and seized many leaders of the League, though he missed the Duc de Mayenne. This scandalous murder of the "King of Paris," as the capital fondly called the Duke, brought the wretched King no solace or power. His mother did not live to see the end of her son; she died in this the darkest period of his career, and must have been aware that her cunning and her immoral life had brought nothing but misery to herself and all her race. The power of the League party seemed as great as ever; the Duc de Mayenne entered Paris, and declared open war on Henri III., who, after some hesitation, threw himself into the hands of his cousin Henri of Navarre in the spring of 1589. The old Politique party now rallied to the King; the Huguenots were stanch for their old leader; things looked less dark for them since the destruction of the Spanish Armada in the previous summer. The Swiss, aroused by the threats of the Duke of Savoy at Geneva, joined the Germans, who once more entered northeastern France; the leaguers were unable to make head either against them or against the armies of the two Kings; they fell back on Paris, and the allies hemmed them in. The defence of the capital was but languid; the populace missed their idol, the Duc de Guise, and the moderate party, never extinguished, recovered strength. All looked as if the royalists would soon reduce the last stronghold of the League, when Henri III. was suddenly slain by the dagger of a fanatical half-wined priest.

The King had only time to commend Henri of Navarre to his courtiers as his heir, and to exhort him to become a Catholic, before he closed his eyes, and ended the long roll of his vices and crimes. And thus in crime and shame the House of Valois went down. For a few years, the throne remained practically vacant: the heroism of Henri of Navarre, the loss of strength in the Catholic powers, the want of a vigorous head to the League,—these things all sustained the Bourbon in his arduous struggle; the middle party grew in strength daily, and when once Henri had allowed himself to be converted, he became the national sovereign, the national favourite, and the high Catholics fell to the fatal position of an unpatriotic faction depending on the arm of the foreigner.

4. The civil wars were not over, for the heat of party raged as yet unslaked; the Politiques could not all at once adopt a Huguenot King, the League party had pledged itself to resist the heretic, and Henri at first had little more than the Huguenots at his back. There were also formidable claimants for the throne. Charles II. Duc de Lorraine, who had married Claude, younger daughter of Henri IL., and who was therefore brother-in-law to Henri III., set up a vague claim; the King of Spain, Philip II., thought that the Salic law had prevailed long enough in France, and that his own wife, the elder daughter of Henri III. had the best claim to the throne; the Guises, though their head was gone, still hoping for the crown, proclaimed their sham-king, the Cardinal de Bourbon, as Charles X., and intrigued behind the shadow of his name. The Duc de Mayenne, their present chief, was the most formidable of Henri's opponents; his party called for a convocation of States General, which should choose a King to succeed, or to replace, their feeble Charles X. During this struggle the high Catholic party, inspired by Jesuit advice, stood forward as the admirers of constitutional principles; they called on the nation to decide the question as to the succession; their Jesuit friends wrote books on the sovereignty of the people. They summoned up troops from every side; the Duc de Lorraine sent his son to resist Henri and support his own claim; the King of Spain sent a body of men; the League princes brought what force they could. Henri of Navarre at the same moment found himself weakened by the silent withdrawal from his camp of the army of Henri III.;

the Politique nobles did not care at first to throw in their lot with the Huguenot chieftain; they offered to confer on Henri the post of commander-in-chief, and to reserve the question as to the succession; they let him know that they recognised his hereditary rights, and were hindered only by his heretical opinions; if he would but be converted they were his. Henri temporised; his true strength, for the time, lay in his Huguenot followers, rugged and faithful fighting men, whose belief was the motive power of their allegiance and of their courage. If he joined the Politiques at their price, the price of declaring himself Catholic, the Huguenots would be offended if not alienated. So he neither absolutely refused nor said yes; and the chief Catholic nobles in the main stood aloof, watching the struggle between Huguenot and Leaguer, as it worked out its course.

Henri, thus weakened, abandoned the siege of Paris, and fell back; with the bulk of his forces he marched into Normandy, so as to be within reach of English succour; a considerable army went into Champagne, to be ready to join any Swiss or German help that might come. These were the great days in the life of Henri of Navarre. Henri showed himself a hero, who strove for a great cause—the cause of European freedom—as well as for his own crown.

The Duc de Mayenne followed the Huguenots down into the west, and found Henri awaiting him in a strong position at Arques, near Dieppe; here at bay, the "Bearnais" inflicted a heavy blow on his assailants; Mayenne fell back into Picardy; the Prince of Lorraine drew off altogether; and Henri marched triumphantly back to Paris, ravaged the suburbs and then withdrew to Tours, where he was recognised as King by the Parliament. His campaign of 1589 had been most successful; he had defeated the League in a great battle, thanks to his skilful use of his position at Arques, and the gallantry of his troops, which more than counterbalanced the great disparity in numbers. He had seen dissension break out among his enemies; even the Pope, Sixtus, had shown him some favour, and the Politique nobles were certainly not going against him. Early in 1590 Henri had secured Anjou, Maine, and Normandy, and in March defeated Mayenne, in a great pitched battle at Ivry, not far from Dreux. The Leaguers fell back in consternation to Paris. Henri reduced all the country round the capital, and sat down before it for a stubborn siege. The Duke of Parma had at that time his hands full in the Low Countries; young Prince Maurice was beginning to show his great abilities as a soldier, and had got possession of Breda; all, however, had to be suspended by the Spaniards on that side, rather than let Henri of Navarre take Paris. Parma with great skill relieved the capital without striking a blow, and the campaign of 1590 ended in a failure for Henri. The success of Parma, however, made Frenchmen feel that Henri's was the national cause, and that the League flourished only by interference of the foreigner. Were the King of Navarre but a

Catholic, he should be a King of France of whom they might all be proud. This feeling was strengthened by the death of the old Cardinal de Bourbon, which reopened at once the succession question, and compelled Philip of Spain to show his hand. He now claimed the throne for his daughter Elisabeth, as eldest daughter of the eldest daughter of Henri II. All the neighbours of France claimed something; Frenchmen felt that it was either Henri IV. or dismemberment. The "Bearnais" grew in men's minds to be the champion of the Salic law, of the hereditary principle of royalty against feudal weakness, of unity against dismemberment, of the nation against the foreigner.

The middle party, the Politiques of Europe,—the English, that is, and the Germans,—sent help to Henri, by means of which he was able to hold his own in the northwest and southwest throughout 1591. Late in the year the violence of the Sixteen of Paris drew on them severe punishment from the Duc de Mayenne; and consequently the Duke ceased to be the recognised head of the League, which now looked entirely to Philip II. and Parma, while Paris ceased to be its headquarters; and more moderate counsels having taken the place of its fierce fanaticism, the capital came under the authority of the lawyers and citizens, instead of the priesthood and the bloodthirsty mob. Henri, meanwhile, who was closely beleaguering Rouen, was again outgeneralled by Parma, and had to raise the siege. Parma, following him westward, was wounded at Caudebec; and though he carried his army triumphantly back to the Netherlands, his career was ended by this trifling wound. He did no more, and died in 1592.

In 1593, Mayenne, having sold his own claims to Philip of Spain, the opposition to Henri looked more solid and dangerous than ever; he therefore thought the time was come for the great step which should rally to him all the moderate Catholics. After a decent period of negotiation and conferences, he declared himself convinced, and heard mass at St. Denis. The conversion had immediate effect; it took the heart out of the opposition; city after city came in; the longing for peace was strong in every breast, and the conversion seemed to remove the last obstacle. The Huguenots, little as they liked it, could not oppose the step, and hoped to profit by their champion's improved position. Their ablest man, Sully, had even advised Henri to make the plunge. In 1594, Paris opened her gates to Henri, who had been solemnly crowned, just before, at Chartres. He was welcomed with immense enthusiasm, and from that day onwards has ever been the favourite hero of the capital. By 1595 only one foe remained,—the Spanish Court. The League was now completely broken up; the Parliament of Paris gladly aided the King to expel the Jesuits from France. In November, 1595, Henri declared war against Spain, for anything was better than the existing state of things, in which Philip's hand secretly supported all opposition: The war in 1596 was far from being successful for Henri; he was comforted, however, by receiving at last the papal absolution, which swept away the last scruples of France.

By rewards and kindliness,—for Henri was always willing to give and had a pleasant word for all, most of the reluctant nobles, headed by the Duc de Mayenne himself, came in in the course of 1596. Still the war pressed very heavily, and early in 1597 the capture of Amiens by the Spaniards alarmed Paris, and roused the King to fresh energies. With help of Sully (who had not yet received the title by which he is known in history) Henri recovered Amiens, and checked the Spanish advance. It was noticed that while the old Leaguers came very heartily to the King's help, the Huguenots hung back in a discontented and suspicious spirit. After the fall of Amiens the war languished; the Pope offered to mediate, and Henri had time to breathe. He felt that his old comrades, the offended Huguenots, had good cause for complaint; and in April, 1598, he issued the famous Edict of Nantes, which secured their position for nearly a century. They got toleration for their opinions; might worship openly in all places, with the exception of a few towns in which the League had been strong; were qualified to hold office in financial posts and in the law; had a Protestant chamber in the Parliaments.

Immediately after the publication of the Edict of Nantes, the Treaty of Vervins was signed. Though Henri by it broke faith with Queen Elizabeth, he secured an honourable peace for his country, an undisputed kingship for himself. It was the last act of Philip II., the confession that his great schemes were unfulfilled, his policy a failure.

Printed in the United Kingdom
by Lightning Source UK Ltd.
101389UKS00001B/335